Awaken from the Dream

A Presentation of *A Course in Miracles*

Gloria and Kenneth Wapnick

Foundation for "ACIM"
RD #2   Box 71
Roscoe,   NY   12776
(607) 498-4116

Cover Art by Lex Reibestein

Portions used by permission from *A Course in Miracles* © 1975,
Foundation for Inner Peace, Inc.

Copyright © 1987 by
Foundation for *"A Course in Miracles,"* Inc.
P.O. Box 783
Crompond, NY 10517

Printed in the United States of America

ISBN: 0-933-291-04-3

Dedication

For two thousand years Jesus and Mary have been symbols of God's unchanging Love for all His children. Knowing that the separation was only a tiny, mad idea they were perfect demonstrations, in an imperfect world, of the Love, grace and unity of Heaven. Their message, lived two thousand years ago and given now in *A Course in Miracles,* offers us a quicker way to return to God. This book is dedicated to the world's acceptance of this message, presented once again in this book, in gratitude to Jesus and Mary who are the loving manifestation of the Holy Spirit.

CONTENTS

PREFACE

Awaken from the Dream is based on the teachings of *A Course in Miracles*. For those reading about the Course for the first time, we begin with a brief account of its origin, nature, and thought system.

How *A Course in Miracles* Came

A Course in Miracles was the result of a collaborative venture of two psychologists, Helen Schucman and William Thetford. They were, respectively, Associate and Full Professors of Medical Psychology at the Columbia-Presbyterian Medical Center in New York City. Bill arrived there in 1957 as the Director of the Psychology Department. In the early part of 1958, Bill hired Helen to head a research project. The first seven years of their relationship were strained, for Helen and Bill were as different as two people could be, a situation exacerbated by the shared perception that each was the source of the other's problems. Yet despite the ambivalence of their relationship, they worked very well together on the professional level. In addition to the usual pressures of academia, there were morale problems within the Department that required their combined attention and efforts. Psychology, as in most medical centers in those days, was considered a black sheep.

A turning point came in the spring of 1965. Just before they were to attend a regular interdisciplinary meeting at another Medical Center in the City, Bill did

1

something very out of character for him: He made a long and impassioned speech to Helen, the gist of which was that he had been giving their relationship and relationships within the Medical Center a great deal of thought. He concluded that there must be a "better way" of relating to others than with the aggression, competition and judgment that so typically characterized their interactions. Equally out of character was Helen's response: She agreed with him. Not knowing what this "better way" was, she nonetheless pledged to join with Bill in trying to find it. We might say that in that instant of joining—what the Course would later call a "holy instant"—the Course was born, even though it would still be a period of several months until it began to be written down.

This collaborative venture of two antagonists— shifting their perception of each other from hate to forgiveness, from separate interests to a shared one—is a shining example of the miracle: "The holiest of all the spots on earth is where an ancient hatred has become a present love" (text, p. 522). Thus we can see how the Course, from its inception, maintained a consistency in exemplifying what it would teach.

It was as if Helen had been waiting for Bill to ask his question, for it triggered a series of internal events—dreams, visions, psychic experiences—that continued on into the autumn of 1965. These were totally unexpected as Helen had steadfastly defined herself as a research psychologist, dedicated to the empirical, "hard-headed" truth she perceived to be the proper domain of the scientist. Thus, there was no room within this role for what she referred to as "soft" or "fuzzy" thinking, which certainly included the psychic and religious experiences that were occurring regularly to her now. Bill, who was Helen's confidant (her husband Louis found these experiences upsetting), likewise had shared Helen's lack of interest in these phenomena, at least up until now. And yet, neither could deny the fact that these events were occurring, especially where they concerned verifiable telepathic experiences.

These experiences drew to a climax in October, 1965, when Helen said to Bill that she thought she was about to do something very unexpected. Bill suggested she get herself a notebook, since she knew shorthand, and write down what she was thinking, hearing, and seeing. Helen proceeded to do this until its culmination one evening later that month when she began to hear an inner voice insistingly repeating: "This is a course in miracles. Please take notes." Frantically she called Bill, who calmly and wisely suggested that she do what the voice said, bring her notes to the office the following morning, and they would see what developed. Seven years later, what had developed were the three books now known as *A Course in Miracles*.

The inner voice identified itself as Jesus, and much of the material is written in the first person. It is not necessary for a student to accept Jesus' authorship to learn and practice the Course's principles, however. As the Course says:

> It is possible to read his words and benefit from them without accepting him into your life. Yet he would help you yet a little more if you will share your pains and joys with him, and leave them both to find the peace of God. Yet still it is his lesson most of all that he would have you learn . . . (manual, p. 84).

However, it is important to accept that the Course states that Jesus is the source of the material:

This course has come from him (Jesus) because his words have reached you in a language you can love and understand (manual, p. 56).

This is particularly important to keep in mind as there are many references to Jesus' crucifixion and resurrection, attempting to correct what the Course sees as the mistakes of traditional Christianity.

Helen's experience of Jesus' dictating voice was of an internal tape recorder that she could turn on or off at will. She did not go into a trance or altered state, or perform automatic writing. Helen was fully conscious and could be interrupted at any time, even in the middle of a sentence, and be able to return and pick up where she left off. This becomes particularly impressive in light of the many sections of the material which are written in iambic pentameter, in complicated Shakespearean blank verse. Usually the dictation came at times that were convenient for Helen, such as the evening, and were not disruptive of her daily routine. Occasionally, if she broke off the dictation before a section was completed, she would not be able to fall asleep until she was done. Each day at the Medical Center, whenever time permitted in their very busy schedules, Helen would dictate to Bill what had been dictated to her the previous day. Bill would type it, at the same time trying to assuage the acute anxiety that made Helen's reading to him so difficult. It was truly, as was stated above, a collaborative venture.

Aside from deletion of personal material given to help Helen and Bill in their own learning, the Course is virtually as it was dictated. Thus, there are not the distortions that crept into Jesus' message so quickly after his death almost two thousand years ago. The text came through without sections and chapters, and without punctuation or paragraphing. The initial work on these was done by Helen and Bill. Two pamphlets were also channeled through Helen in similar fashion: "Psychotherapy: Purpose, Process and Practice," a summary of the Course's principles of healing as applied to the profession of psychotherapy; and "The Song of Prayer," a poetic summary of the Course's teachings on forgiveness and healing.*

Helen had difficulty applying the principles of the Course to all facets of her life, though—contrary to the distorted accounts that have already begun to appear—she never doubted the Course's truth, nor that Jesus was the source of the material. In fact, she was always quite protective of the Course's purity, understanding it from deep within herself, and critical of those who distorted its teachings and sought to use the Course for personal gain. She could always discern authenticity from inauthenticity and, to quote her favorite play *Hamlet*, knew "a hawk from a handsaw."

Rumors again to the contrary, Helen was never truly an atheist, although she did pose as one during the beginning of her professional career. Born Jewish, she had been a spiritual seeker since childhood with a special attraction to Roman Catholicism, though never subscribing to its doctrines or dogmas. Her love-hate relationship with the Church extended to Jesus, and she finally abandoned her quest in frustration and anger, believing that she had done her part in seeking God, but that He had not done His. Helen's struggles

*These are available, along with *A Course in Miracles*, from the Foundation for Inner Peace, Box 635, Tiburon, CA 94920.

with Jesus, incidentally, can be seen in some of the poems she had taken down, published posthumously by the Foundation for Inner Peace as *The Gifts of God*.

What is almost as impressive as *A Course in Miracles* were Helen and Bill themselves. Helen asked Jesus shortly after the dictation began why she was doing this instead of a holy nun, or someone seemingly more suited to this role. He answered her simply: "Because you would do it." And since she was already "doing it," she could not argue with him. However, Helen and Bill were excellent for their roles, not only because they would complete the dictation, but because they would do it with integrity and faithfulness. Their joint dedication was a true example of purity of intention, of fidelity to what Bill once called a "sacred trust." Regardless of the personal and professional ego interferences that are present in all of us, Helen and Bill never allowed them to enter into their work with the Course, both during the dictation itself as well as afterwards. One could not have asked for two more faithful participants in the Holy Spirit's plan of salvation.

What *A Course in Miracles* Is

A Course in Miracles consists of three books—text, workbook for students, and manual for teachers—and is thus presented as a learning curriculum. It should be noted that it states that we are all teachers and students alike, so the three books are meant for all people who become students of the Course. The text provides the theoretical foundation for the practical application of its ideas found in the workbook, which consists of three hundred and sixty-five lessons, one for each day of the year. While very few "rules" are given in the material, and there is no suggested order for working with any of the books, it is important that any serious student of the material study all three books at some point. Without the text, the ideas given in the workbook would be meaningless and easily misunderstood, while omitting the very specific practical applications of the daily workbook lessons would render the text's teachings mere abstractions. The third volume is the manual for teachers, and consists of questions and answers which summarize some of the more important themes found in the Course. An appendix to the manual includes a clarification of some of the Course's terms; this was taken down three years after the Course itself was completed.

Despite the three hundred and sixty-five lessons of the workbook, the Course is not a "one year" curriculum. The workbook closes with the following words, hardly reassuring to a student with hopes of having all problems magically removed after the final lessons: "This course is a beginning, not an end" (workbook, p. 477). The purpose of the workbook is merely to re-orient our thinking along the principles of the text, helping us spend the rest of our lives assimilating its teachings and, under the guidance of our Teacher, the Holy Spirit, learning the lessons our daily experiences present to us.

The Course makes no claim to being the only form of truth, nor the only spiritual path a person may choose back to God. In fact, it states that it is only one form "of the universal course . . . (among) many thousands of other forms, all with the same outcome" (manual, p. 3). Thus, despite sharing a common goal, all spiritualities can be seen to have certain unique aspects that distinguish them from each other. *A Course in*

Miracles is not only unique but radical, in its etymological sense of going to the root of things. It repeatedly urges us to return to the root or original cause of our problems: the belief in our separation from God.

A Course in Miracles teaches that the way to remember the God who created us is by undoing our guilt through forgiving others and therefore ourselves. Its focus is thus on the healing of relationships. It is unusual in its integration of a non-dualistic metaphysics with a practical psychology. In this regard, one of the most important statements the Course makes is that God, being a loving Creator, did not create this world. Far from leaving this idea as an abstract theological issue with no relevance to our daily lives, the Course helps us recognize the extraordinary personal implications of this truth. In fact, one could say that without acceptance of this metaphysical premise, students would not be fully able to understand the Course's theoretical system, let alone apply its practical teachings on forgiveness to every area of their lives, without exception. Thus, the metaphysical statements on the nature of God and the world are integrated with a sophisticated psychology that helps us to understand and apply its ontological teachings to our individual salvation.

Thus, on the one hand the Course teaches that God did not create the physical world, which therefore is seen as not real but illusory: the result of our mistake in believing we had separated from God. On the other hand it emphasizes the importance of living in this world *as if* it were real, experiencing it as a classroom in which we learn our lessons of forgiveness. These lessons ultimately generalize to all our relationships, up to and including God. We awaken from the dream of separation as our mistaken thought system is corrected, and we are returned to the awareness of our Source in Heaven.

The Course is also unique in its interesting blend of Eastern and Western thought. Its non-dualistic metaphysics has more parallels in the ancient teachings of Hinduism and Buddhism than in the dualistic thinking of the major Western religions. Yet the Course's language is Judaeo-Christian, while its psychology is largely derived from the pioneering work of Sigmund Freud.

The Course's universal spiritual vision, therefore, has come within specific sectarian forms, and has led to the obvious question: If the Course is non-sectarian in its theme, why would its statement be Christian, with Jesus' identity as the source of the material so explicit? The Course itself states: "A universal theology is impossible, but a universal experience is not only possible but necessary" (manual, p. 73). Interestingly enough, the Course's "Christianity" has presented problems for Jewish and Christian readers alike, not to mention those spiritual seekers who do not feel connected to any specific religious form. The answer to this question is found in the basic methodology of the Course itself: correcting our errors in the forms in which they appear. The Course teaches that forgiveness can only heal within the form in which the unforgiveness was expressed. By joining us in the world of our mistakes, the Course gently corrects our illusions and leads us beyond them to the truth.

To even the most casual observer, it is clear that the most dominant element throughout two thousand years of Western history has been Christianity, and this influence has found its way into every major aspect of our society. Our years are numbered from the presumed birth of Jesus, and not a person, regardless of his or her religion, has failed to be influenced by Jesus and the religions that took his name. It is also apparent that Christianity has not been very Christian. Nietzsche remarked that "in truth, there was only *one* Christian and he died on the cross," while Chesterton has noted that the Christian ideal "has not been tried and found wanting; it has been found difficult and left untried."

One need not be a keen student of history, therefore, to realize that Christianity's gifts to the world have been double-edged. On the one hand, it preserved for centuries the memory and example of Jesus—the purest expression we have known of the love of God—including his gospel of forgiveness, as well as benefitting the world with its many cultural and artistic contributions. On the other hand, Christianity has been a religion of sacrifice, guilt, persecution, murder and elitism, with Jesus its primary symbol—he whose gospel was only love, forgiveness, peace and unity. As the Course states: "Some bitter idols have been made of him who would be only brother to the world" (manual, p. 84). The development of Christianity can be seen in part as the history of a people who, though believing in Jesus and his message, often unwittingly brought conflict, war and separation instead of peace, unity and salvation to the world. Rather than viewing all people as one family under God, it has divided and subdivided this family. Before we can fully accept this radical message of forgiveness and the oneness of *all* people as God's family, the errors of the past must be corrected and undone. As the

Course makes clear, the errors of Christianity are merely reflective of the basic errors of any person or group that believes that the separation from God has actually occurred. Christianity thus affords us the opportunity of not only healing the errors of the past, but of understanding better the dynamics of our own egos through seeing them in the history of the Christian religions.

Those who begin the Course expecting to find—for better or worse—the Christianity they had learned and practiced, or the Christianity that seemed to condone bigotry and persecution, will be very much surprised. They will find many of the words they were familiar with—atonement, salvation, forgiveness of sins, Christ, Son of God, etc.—but with different meanings and connotations. The crucifixion remains the central event in Jesus' life, yet the Course's interpretation is 180 degrees from the traditional teaching that he suffered and died for our sins. Moreover, the crucifixion is explained as a forgiveness model for our own behavior when we are tempted to perceive ourselves unfairly treated by the world.

While Freud generally receives a "bad press" in popular as well as many professional circles—in part because of his strong anti-religious attitude—it is nonetheless true that without his work there could not have been *A Course in Miracles*. The dynamics of the ego, as presented by the Course, are largely psychoanalytic, and certainly the widespread acceptance and understanding of projection is directly attributable to his work and those who followed in his footsteps. Paradoxically, then, we can observe that the insights of the man who strove so passionately to deny the existence of spirituality can be turned around to help us undo the ego barriers that have kept us from recognizing our true identities as children of God.

Finally, it is important to note that the Course came into the world in a most unlikely place—a large medical center in the heart of New York City. One could not have asked for a more dramatic setting to symbolize the materialism and misuse of power in our world. As we already have observed regarding Christianity, errors need to be corrected in the forms in which they are expressed. For those who would be tempted to "practice" or "learn" the Course in isolation, the Course's birthplace serves as a symbolic reminder of the necessity of learning our lessons right where we are, in the problematic relationships and daily situations of our lives. The Course states:

> *There are those who are called upon to change their life situation almost immediately, but these are generally special cases. By far the majority are given a slowly-evolving training program, in which as many previous mistakes as possible are corrected. Relationships in particular must be properly perceived, and all dark cornerstones of unforgiveness removed* (manual, p. 25).

AUTHORS' NOTE

Kenneth

I grew up in a Jewish home in Brooklyn, New York and, after a thorough Hebew elementary school education, decided at the age of thirteen that I had had my fill, not only with Judaism but with all religion. I entered into an extended period of agnosticism, which paralleled an increasing involvement in the world of classical music. Among others, Beethoven and Mozart were my guides who ultimately led me to recognize that there was indeed a God who created and loved me. Along the way, I completed my doctoral studies in clinical psychology (1968), which included a dissertation on the mystical experiences of St. Teresa of Avila, a 16th century Spanish Catholic.

After the breakup of my first marriage in 1970, I took a job as Chief Psychologist in a New York State mental hospital. Despite my active involvement in hospital affairs during this two year period, I lived as a very private person, increasingly drawn to a simpler way of living which I later identified with monasticism. Reading the Trappist monk Thomas Merton in the Spring of 1972 eventually led me to his monastery, the Abbey of Gethsemani, in Kentucky. To my great surprise I was very much at home there, and experienced the same direct presence of God that I felt when listening to Beethoven or Mozart. I therefore concluded that it was God's Will that I become a monk and a Catholic.

I acted quickly and soon after was baptized in September, 1972, not only *not* believing in the teachings of the Church, but not really caring about its central figure. It was not until several months later that Jesus became central to my life. I did, however, feel very much drawn to the monastery, and planned to enter upon waiting the one year the Church mandated after a baptism. I left my hospital job two months later, Thanksgiving week, 1972, and prepared to leave for Israel not even sure why I was going.

Shortly before I left, a priest-psychologist friend of mine suggested I meet two psychologists—Helen Schucman and William Thetford—whom he said were also very much involved in spirituality. We spent a pleasant evening together and, while nothing was said about the Course which they had only just completed taking down, mention was made of a book that Helen "had written." Bill had then pointed to his living room corner and the stack of seven large thesis binders which to that date housed the Course. I declined their offer to look at the manuscript, as I did not think I should begin such a large undertaking just as I was about to leave for Israel. But I did think about the book for the next five months I was in Israel, most of which time was unexpectedly spent in two monasteries.

I came back to New York in May, 1973, planning only to remain about a month before returning to a monastery atop a mountain in Galilee. Things worked out differently, however. I visited Helen and Bill shortly after my return and saw the Course for the first time. I soon realized that this was what I had been looking for without knowing I had been looking for it. *A Course in Miracles* was the only system I had ever seen that fully integrated psychology and spirituality, doing full justice to both, and the presence of Jesus in the material dovetailed with my finally accepting his presence in my life. Moreover, I recognized that Helen and Bill were the spiritual family I had been searching for as well. We became close personal friends and I remained in New York, joining them at the Medical Center. A substantial part of our early years together was spent in carefully reviewing the manuscript— checking punctuation, capitalization, paragraphing, and section and chapter titles. We met Judith Skutch in 1975 and, through our combined efforts, the Course was published in 1976 under the aegis of the Foundation for Inner Peace.

Gloria

I was born Roman Catholic, and grew up in the Bronx, New York. Being religious as a child, I yearned in my heart to enter a convent, but never spoke of this to anyone. I enjoyed being in Church the most when no services were being held, and I could kneel or sit by the altar of Mary and pour out my deepest feelings to her. It was as if she were my mother, and I could always feel her comforting and loving presence surrounding me. This changed radically, however, after spending a year in Italy with my mother and sister when I was thirteen. Hearing firsthand about the devastating effects World War II had on people personally, I concluded that if this world were the best that God could create, I wanted nothing more to do with Him. I thought to myself—What kind of God is this?

When I returned to the States I sought out members of the clergy for help in my dilemma, but the theological (and psychological) explanations that were given to me were unsatisfying. And so I left God and the Church. Feeling empty inside, I eventually began a long spiritual search that included Hinduism, Buddhism and Rosicrucianism, but though I found much in these and other paths that were interesting and helpful, there remained "something missing" that I could not account for.

In the meantime I had two unhappy marriages that led to divorce, had two children, and lived and taught in Iran for two and half years. Back in the States, I acquired a Master's in History and taught for over 17 years, mostly in a New York City high school. The last four of these years I doubled as Dean of Students.

In 1977, at the recomendation of a colleague, I saw Pat Rodegast, a psychic then living in Connecticut. Her spirit-guide, Emmanuel, among many useful and helpful things, told me to go to Wainwright House (a New Age conference center in Rye, New York) and there I would find what I had been looking for all my life. At that point I was not even sure what I was looking for, and was rather surprised at such a statement. Moreover, I had never even heard of Wainwright House but, being intrigued, located it and went to a week-end symposium on healing.

The workshop I attended was on *A Course in Miracles*. I returned home that first evening with the books, and almost consumed the early chapters of the text. For the first time in many years I could feel Jesus' presence. From the opening pages of the text I could almost hear his voice in the very words themselves. As I read Jesus' words explain that God did not create the world, it was as if "lightning bolts" crashed through my head. "Why hadn't I thought of that?" I kept thinking to myself. "It is so simple; that is the answer." Finally, after twenty-three years the puzzle in my mind was solved. The Course had supplied the missing piece, and I no longer had to blame God for a world He did not create. Yet without the gently authoritative presence of Jesus behind the Course's words I doubt I would have accepted this idea so readily.

This experience changed my entire life and, eager to share this material with others, I began a weekly study group in my home shortly afterwards. This helped to deepen my understanding of the Course's teaching, on both theoretical and practical levels. Kenneth and I met in 1978, although I had heard him speak a year before then, and we were married in

1981. We began the Foundation for "A Course in Miracles" in 1983, and I left teaching in 1984 to devote myself full-time to the Foundation and to speaking about the Course.

In the beginning of 1986 I began to have a series of internal auditory and visual experiences that enabled me to glimpse the pre-separation state of Heaven's Love and peace, the painful instant of separation, and the consequences that ultimately resulted in the making of the physical universe. The experiences reflected very powerfully my own struggles in practicing the Course's teaching on total forgiveness, with no opposition to illusion in any of its forms. In sharing the experience with some friends, and in a limited form in workshops, I found that though the experience itself was very personal, it did seem to have application to others. It provided a context in which to better understand the interface between the Course's metaphysical vision and its practical application in our individual lives.

Thus when Kenneth and I decided to write a book on the Course we felt we should begin with a statement of this experience. While the power of this experience reflected truth for me it may not necessarily do that for others. Thus we have presented it in mythological form in the hope that it can be of help towards a more personal understanding of the abstract nature of the Course's thought system. The mythological figures, as in any myth, can become helpful symbols for individuals on a spiritual journey.

The Voice of the Light group that is presented in the myth, calling to those who believed in the reality of the separation to awaken from their dream, was personified for me in Jesus and his mother Mary. Since those specific identities are not necessary for others they have not been mentioned in the myth. My vision was that Jesus and Mary, though they separated along with the rest of the Sonship, never bought into the reality of the dream. This differs from the Course teaching that, like us, Jesus had lessons to learn. Mary, meanwhile, is not discussed anywhere in the Course. I mention this at the outset so as not to confuse the student or future student of the Course. This difference, though personally important to me, remains irrelevant to the message of the Light group and to the theme of this book.

INTRODUCTION

Almost all of the world's religions contain a story or myth that seeks to describe the origin of the world and our purpose in being here. Down through the ages, the myth has been an instructive tool for expressing experiences that often seem to be beyond more objective description. *A Course in Miracles* too has a mythic framework, which attempts to render understandable what can never be truly understood. The Course reflects the story of how a part of the Son of God fell asleep and, believing he had a will that could oppose the Will of God, dreamed that he could separate from his Creator and usurp His throne. Yet, the truth remains that we "are at home in God, dreaming of exile but perfectly capable of awakening to reality" (text, p. 169). It was our failure to awaken from the dream of rebellion that set into motion the cosmic drama that culminated in the making of the physical universe. Furthermore, it is our ongoing failure to awaken from our individual dreams that compels us to repeat this "drama" of separation in each and every aspect of our dreaming in this world. Forgiveness becomes the means that the Holy Spirit, God's Answer to the separation, uses to correct the Son's misthought and reunite the fragmented Sonship.

The present book is a discussion of the basic principles of *A Course in Miracles*. It is based on Gloria's experience, discussed in the Preface, which fleshes out the mythic framework of the Course. The myth presents the experience of the pre- and post-separation states, the psychological events that led to the making of the world, and the ultimate acceptance of the Holy Spirit's message which awakens the Sonship from its dream of separation and returns it Home. The opening chapter will present this mythological rendering of what the Course reminds us we have blotted out of awareness. The succeeding chapters discuss the issues raised in the myth which constitute the essence of the Course.

This book, however, does not aim at an in-depth look at *A Course in Miracles*; for that, the reader may consult *Forgiveness and Jesus* (published by the Foundation for "A Course in Miracles"). Rather, *Awaken from the Dream*'s purpose is twofold: to introduce the Course to those who are new to it; as well as to provide for those who are already its students, another lens through which to approach and understand the Course's thought system.

Chapter 1

THE MYTH

I—HEAVEN

Come with us on a journey of discovery to the remembrance of who we are. Sink back into your mind, and let yourself be carried out of time and out of this world into another dimension, whose glorious splendor language cannot express. Yet must we use words to reflect the ineffable Reality that is beyond all words, in order to recall to our minds the radiant abstraction of Heaven which has been replaced by our world of concrete specifics.

Our memory leads us back to this state of Holiness where, in the Beginning, before there was even a concept of beginning, there is God, our Source and the Source of all creation: a perfection and resplendence whose magnificence is beyond comprehension; love and gentleness of such an infinite nature that consciousness could not even begin its apprehension; a pristine stillness of uninterrupted joy, a motionless flow without friction to impede it; a vast, limitless and all-encompassing Totality, beyond space, beyond time, in which there is no beginning, no ending, for there was never a time or place when God was not.

God our Source is the All, and shares this Totality with us. This is a sharing without limits, and with no withholding of what truly is. Therefore, as part of our Source, we share all Its qualities, even unto being a co-creator.

Creation, like spirit, is abstract, formless and un-

21

changing. Its nature is unity, knowledge of which is that there is nowhere the Creator ends and the created begins. There is no boundary, no differentiation, no separation. Yet, included in this knowledge is the fact that we are not the Source of creation, though we remain one within It.

Can the Mind of God begin? Can the Mind of God end? Can a Thought that is part of that Mind be something other than that Mind? Surely not, since there is no subject or object in the state of Heaven; no observer or observed. There is no perception, simply the total knowledge of who we are: a glory of such unified resplendence that concepts of within-without have no meaning.

We are an Idea in the Mind of God, and this Idea, with no limitations, is composed of an infinite number of Thoughts. All these Thoughts are the Sons of God, and the unified Idea—the Christ—*is* the Son. Therefore, all God's Thoughts are creation and, since Mind extends, the unlimited Thoughts the Mind of God extends are the Christ. We are the formless Thoughts that pulsate from this vast Mind, yet these Thoughts are abstract and have no counterpart to the specific forms in our world. As Thoughts in God's Mind, we emulate the process of creation, and our extensions are our creations.

We know our Creator-Source and have total gratitude for being part of the All. Gratitude is a constant song sung by the created to its Source, in glad thanksgiving for the knowledge of its Holiness as part of the Source. God's Being is Love, and Love, without end, flows continually between Creator and created, unbroken and uninterrupted. It is the Source of all Being, and is itself all Being. Love is the very fountainhead of

God, the essence of spirit and Mind, from which the Great Rays of resplendence radiate all that belongs to the Kingdom: truth, joy, unity and peace.

This is Reality, our true inheritance as children of our Source who says that all that I have is yours. Totally at rest, the Son is home in the knowledge within the Mind that created it. This is the Reality God established, forever changeless, forever perfect. This is His eternal truth: God is; His Sons are one with Him in perfect love, innocence and peace.

II—THE DESCENT INTO HELL

Suddenly out of nowhere a thought seemingly occurred within the mind of one of the Sons of God: "Can there be an opposite to what is?" One component-Son, a part of the All, wanted to experience being the All, the Source of all Being, and to deny and replace our Source. Inherent in this thought was limiting the limitless, forming the formless, concretizing abstraction, and the making of specifics; in short, a rejection of our Creator-Source and creation as established by Him; a thought inconceivable in reality yet somehow conceived.

This madness, this tiny, mad idea—"Can there be an opposite to what is?"—laser beamed throughout the Sonship like an infectious virus. It was experienced as a thundrous crash that shattered the stillness of Heaven and seemed to cast the Sons of God out of the Kingdom into a dimension of darkness and void. It was as if a partial region of the mind of the Sonship, like a thin layer of cellophane, lifted off into nowhere. A dissonant cacaphony of sound seemed to emerge:

"I have disrupted the All because I have established my own self-creation. I have become my own creator, my own source. I want to be concrete, specific and special. I will limit the vast limitlessness and will structure the formless. I will blot out the totality of love and encapsulate it into the individual, specific and concrete."

Even in this void, the awareness remained in the Sonship that we could not do this in Reality, although we could *believe* ourselves to be in an alternate dimension. Using the power of our Source we believed that we could deny our Source. It was like a great experiment in an alternate reality. Yet we knew that it could not be done in that perfect state of Love and Holiness, and so in order to enthrone ourselves as creator we had to leave the Kingdom. Only by separating and denying our Source, opposing the essence of love, could we believe this could be accomplished. The outcome of this experiment made it seem as if there were an inherent flaw in creation and the Godhead which rendered God impotent and imperfect, and thus perverted creation.

I, as one of the components of the Sonship, experienced these thoughts, which seemed to be like a downward spiral, crescendoing at a pitch of violent intensity. It was an experience of sheer terror and intense fear; emotions of loss and bereavement, unparalleled since they had never been experienced before. Certainty was gone, knowledge had vanished, and I did not understand. What was happening? Where was I? What was I? I thought to myself that this experience of the void—non-being, non-spirit—was the other, the opposite of our Home and of Love. Unity had disappeared for me; where all had been one, opaque forms now began to appear, and I now perceived many separated component-Sons of God.

III—THREE GROUPS

Three groups of opaque thought-forms seemed to be emerging: a Light group, the manifestation of God's Holy Spirit; a dark group that contained the original thought of separation, identifying with it; and finally a middle group, somehow caught between the two. For some reason, the now separated or individual components of the Sonship seemed to be almost electro-magnetically attracted to one of these three groups. I found myself in the middle group.

I had become infected with ignorance, and in my losing total knowledge I believed that this separation thought was possible of accomplishment. The shock of the crossover, out of Heaven into a void, produced this intensity of pain, fear and forgetting.

"Who is responsible for these thoughts of insanity?" I cried out, "How did I end up here?"

In response I heard loud, derisive laughter, and recognized the dark group at once. That original thought, having now appeared in opaquish form, joined with other component-Sons. These thought forms seemed to be thinking:

"We have accomplished the impossible and the inconceivable: self-creation! We have given birth to something that is totally separate from Reality. We have usurped and wrested the power of God, and we have made our selves in our own image. Now *we* are Gods: self-creating and self-created. Our experiment has been accomplished. Moreover, we know that our Source cannot stop us because It shares all power with

25

us. We have accomplished what we wanted by disengaging from the Kingdom. God cannot be Everything because He cannot stop part of Him from separating off. We denied the Cause Its Effects and thus have denied Him His very existence. We have obliterated God!"

Sheer terror engulfed me and I cried out to them: "You are all mad. It is impossible to deny our Source."

But they countered: "Of course we can. Our Source does not stop us. Behold! Our experiment is accomplished!"

I was confused and bewildered: "How can a component-Son come to the awareness that it can deny its Source? Are they trying to tempt God to stop them?" My terror made their boasts appear to be true, but in some other region of my mind I knew that it was impossible. I was experiencing as real what could not be real, and I did not understand. It was quite obvious that they did not care about the Kingdom, because their single consciousness was total opposition to truth, and their intention was to exist in a dimension opposite to Heaven and God.

Thoroughly desperate and distraught, I looked around for help and perceived a great Light emanating from what appeared to be some other thought forms. I went towards this group of Light and pleaded for help and understanding. In the presence of Love surrounding me, I felt a calm assurance from these great Beings who, though aware of that silly, mad idea, had not been contaminated by it because they had never lost the memory of their loving Source. It was as if an unbroken line of Heaven's Light lifted off with them, enabling them to be a continuous presence of Love. A gentle Voice spoke to me from these resplendent thought forms:

26

"Do not be afraid. Remember whence you came and who you are. These silly ideas of usurpation, rebellion and limitation that shattered your peace and joy cannot touch you if you maintain the pure awareness of our Source. What you are experiencing is only a delusion of the mind, and in Reality it can have no real effect."

But I said to them: "Why do I feel so lost: bereft, bewildered, in pain and confused?"

"Remember," the Voice said, "Think back to your first response to that tiny, mad idea that perhaps there could be an opposite to Heaven."

I could not fight off my resistance to that memory, and recognized to my horror what my very first response had been:

"That seems interesting; I wonder what that would be like?"

I grew sickened by the idea that, having considered the possibility of something other than Heaven—if only for a split second—I had allowed that thought to contaminate part of me. The loving Voice of Light explained to me:

"This is the reason for your pain and confusion. A part of your mind that had considered that thought is now experiencing its effects. That is all that has happened. Nothing more. That thought and its effects seem very real to you, but your true state of being—spirit, at one with God—is your *only* Reality. A part of your mind believes that it is experiencing non-reality, a state called consciousness that perceives opposites and duality, in contrast to the unity of Heaven."

"But how can this be?" I exclaimed.

"In truth it isn't," they replied. "Focus your mind now on the remembrance of truth. Hold only to the thought of our Source."

27

But impatiently I said to them:

"We have to do something. We just cannot allow this to go on! We must stop and eradicate this thought of separation and all its consequences."

I was terrified. Painfully I began a mental inventory and realized that through the birth of what we call consciousness I perceived duality, and this became the state of mind of the middle group, myself included. Fear, which I had experienced as a sonic-boom noise, became the first emotion I felt in believing I had separated from my Source, denying the emotion of Heaven, which is Love. This was followed by the perception of the seeming shattering of the unity, fragmenting into many forms. I became even more frightened and could not accept the reassurances of the Light group. The experience of guilt and terror was too strong, and suddenly in my tortured mind I again heard the contemptuous laughter of the dark group. I turned my attention back to them as they said to me:

"How can you listen to what they are telling you? You know what you are experiencing. They do not understand it. Behold! We will show you what power we have."

I turned back to the Light group and, as I felt myself slipping into darkness, screamed to them in desperation:

"Don't you know what they are going to do, what their intentions are? How can you stand there and do nothing? Don't you even care? What they are doing is unforgivable, and so is your allowing it to happen."

With the calmness of Heaven, the Light beings said to me:

"Do not oppose. Do not hold them responsible and do not believe what you are hearing. You know that Love, our true state, can never oppose. Love simply is and there can be no opposite. What appears as opposite is unreal and therefore insane. Do not believe in what does not exist."

I frantically looked about and saw that there were others, like myself, who felt terrified and lost. My thoughts flew to them as their painful plight reinforced my own. I turned again to the Light group, pleading with them:

"Please join with us. Let us all together stop the dark ones so we can flee from this state of separation and return to our Source and Creator. In His holy Name, I urge you to mobilize with us together against the dark ones."

Their loving and authoritative Voice answered:

"Consider this: By opposing these thoughts you are separating yourself from the Sonship and will then make the separation real in your mind, not to mention your own guilt for having first been interested in these thoughts. By giving them this power, you will believe that their insanity is now possible of accomplishment. *If these thoughts truly had no reality for you, you would not bother to oppose them.* Making them real in your mind, you will not be able to avoid becoming part of what will inevitably follow. Remember that you are one with our Source, and all that He has is yours."

I pondered these thoughts and tried to get clarity within as chaos surrounded and engulfed me, pulling me into a downward vortex of terror and self-hatred. I was aware that others were plummeting down this spiral of fear and guilt with me, and in this void of darkness I frantically called out to to those as bewildered as I:

"Let us join together. We now know that the

Light group will not help us, for reasons that are not clear to me. We must act on our own. Together we will oppose the dark components and prevent their evil designs against the Kingdom and our Creator. We can defeat the dark ones in our own way."

And so the battle lines were formed. I joined with other components and together we led the forces of this middle group who wanted to go back to that pristine stillness of Heaven. I was not yet aware that having turned my back on the message of the beings of Light I had entrapped myself, and those who followed me as well, into an unreality that was a denial of the true God and a further descent into hell.

IV—THE MAKING OF THE WORLD: GOD'S FIRST LIEUTENANTS

As I have said, three distinct groups had emerged: the Light beings who did not join with us and oppose; the dark beings who luxuriated in the power wrested from their Source; and the middle group who took it upon themselves to defend God and defeat the dark ones.

I now realized I had developed a divided mind, unlike members of the other two groups. The dark group was singleminded in its intention to experiment and replace God, while the Light group retained only the single memory of God's Love, realizing all else was simply fantasy. As a member of the middle group, I found myself in a paradoxical dilemma. I recognized the truth of the state of mind of the Light group, while I was panic-stricken of the designs of the dark group. The great conflict I felt ripped me in two, and terror gripped my mind.

Reflecting now, I can understand that having appointed myself as God's First Lieutenant, in battle with the forces of darkness, I had fallen into a self-made pit of hell. Making myself into this image of God's spokesperson, defending Him and His Kingdom, I had plunged myself still further into separation. In hindsight I realize that God needs no defense, nor does His Kingdom. Truth is, and what appears as what is not is simply a delusion of the mind. At that point I did not realize how gripped by illusions my mind truly was. The intentions of the dark group preoccupied me for I recognized that they wanted to make the opposite of Heaven, a world whose foundation was the death of the living God. And unwittingly I became instrumental in helping them do just that.

As the dark group continued to revel in their "triumph," my fear-driven mind raged at them in angry protest and opposition. Yet they continued their derisive and defiant laughter:

"You still do not understand the power that we have. We will make the infinite finite, the limitless limited, and the abstract concrete and specific."

They then proceeded to project outward from their mind the thought of their great experiment, and quickly we marshalled the forces of those who followed us to send forth a thought of light to counteract that thought of darkness. As we did so, I beheld the formation of the cosmos, like a Big Bang. I was dumbfounded! The "light" that we sent out against the dark, like two titans clashing, had been incorporated into the darkness as lights—now called stars and planets.

The words from the Light group came back to me, like a truth penetrating the very core of my being.

"Do not oppose. . . . By opposing these thoughts you will then make them real in your mind . . . (and) you will not be able to avoid becoming part of what will inevitably follow."

In that one instant, enlightenment dawned on my mind and I fully understood the truth. Words cannot begin to express the depth and poignancy of my sadness. I painfully realized the tragic mistake I had made. How deeply sorrowful I was! I had compounded my mistake of turning away from Love: first by entertaining for a split second the possibility of there being something opposite to Heaven; and then appointing myself as the Guardian of Truth, although my own foundation was a lie. I beheld that my "holy" purpose—to defend God—was the very denial of Him I was trying to honor and uphold. I became aware that this was indeed the denial of knowledge, and I had fallen into the hypnotic trap of ignorance.

Now that my mind beheld the beginnings of the cosmos, I urgently tried to stop the middle group's opposition to the self-fashioned forces of power, hellbent on attacking God and making a world the opposite of Heaven. I put up my arms and cried out:

"Listen! The great beings of Light were right. By opposing the intentions of the dark ones we have made the error of their thinking real by believing in it. We cannot oppose them because our true nature is Love, and Love does not condemn or oppose. Besides, since they are part of the Sonship we would only be attacking ourselves by attacking them. We must leave this battlefield at once. Please follow me. This time I will not lead you astray. I beg you, come away from this insanity before you become hopelessly engulfed in this delusional madness."

But I was too late. Many in the middle group had already become enmeshed in the power-world of opposition, and said in response to me:

"Leave us be. Don't you know that we are fighting the cause of God and His righteousness? We are the true sons of light because we care about what is happening, in contrast to you and your companions. We will use all our God-given powers to defeat the forces of evil."

But I kept pleading with them:

"Don't you see what is happening? The dark group needs an opposition to their thought of opposition to God, and we are furnishing that for them. If we don't oppose them, these thoughts can have no effects and will vanish into nothingness. But if we do oppose, as we have begun to do, the outcome is that nothing will become something; the tiny, mad idea of separation from our Source and from each other will become forever fixed in our minds. Please listen to me who fell but has recognized my mistake. In the name of the living God and the Christ you are, I urge you to cease your opposition."

Some were moved by what I said and came away with me, going towards the beings of Light. Many others remained, however, delighting in their newly found power. Feeling helpless to prevent them from madly rushing into a hell of their own making, we beheld the miscreation of the physical world, whose rhythm was like point-counterpoint. As the dark forces projected each thought, it was counter-projected by the middle group who believed, in their ignorance, that the total denial of God had already been accomplished. In that conflict and opposition the entire world of matter was built up, step by step: first the greater cosmos, followed

33

by the mineral, vegetable and animal kingdoms: all the so-called life forms everywhere in the universe.

As each projection was emitted from the minds of both groups in combat, I beheld the power of each component-mind lessening. This had to be the case because the making of the world was the opposite of Heaven, where power is never diminished. It was not until near the end of the process that the two groups became aware that their power was getting trapped in the forms they were making. It was the middle group that first became aware of this phenomenon. Perceiving that the power of the dark group had almost spent itself, they wanted to make a creature that they could project themselves into, for that would give them dominion over all that was made. This creature, a so-called sentient being encased in a dense, material body—self-proclaimed as homo sapiens on this planet (hardly conforming to its title)—was the crowning achievement of the middle group's last attempt to wrest the initiative from the dark group. In response, the dark group also projected what little power it had left into these sentient creatures. This was the only time that the point-counterpoint process changed its rhythm, insofar as the middle group took the initiative in this grandiose design of miscreation.

We beheld the carrying out of the dark group's grand experiment. They had learned that the opposite of Heaven's unity was conflict, and therefore opposition was the ingredient that would give their experiment form and provide the material witness to its accomplishment. Thus, their strategy was to take advantage of the middle group's ignorance of what was really happening, playing on their fear, anger and lust for power, goading them to opposition. It was the first seduction, and the middle group fell for the trap of believing that by opposing and triumphing over the dark ones, perceived to be outside, they could avoid the responsibility of confronting the darkness of their own separation thinking, which was only ignorance. I could see so clearly that they were arrogantly using the power of their mind to hate, under the self-righteous guise of love and truth. And I knew they were doomed.

Thus was a world of opposites made from the opposition and clash of the middle and dark group; a material world of density, conflict and hatred. It was in truth a clash of nothing with nothing—one projected thought of separation opposing another projected thought of separation—that produced the world.

Inherent within this distorted perceptual realm that *is* the material universe, time was the mechanism that seemed to bring about the final destruction of the Son of God and all he made. Since the intent behind the making of the world and the body was the opposite of Love, what appeared to be born was intense self-hatred of a nature so gross that not one part of the contaminated Sonship could behold the totality of this self-hatred without intense terror. Thus, the awareness of this intense self-hatred was blotted out of consciousness, but this self-hatred or guilt still unconsciously dictated the multiplicity of dramas that each component-entity would experience through its seemingly endless cycles of birth, death and rebirth.

The apprehension of space duality—subject and object—was immediate after the separation, but the dimension of time was an illusion that was born to engender credence to the idea of destructibility, and to seem to imprint forever the seemingly endless replay in all shapes and forms of the self-hatred or guilt of the components who had been trapped in a delusionary state of mind. We made up time to root our consciousness here, and let it appear that this separation had indeed been accomplished. Therefore, the dark group could boast: "God cannot destroy what He created, but we can destroy what we have made. Therefore, we are greater than God. God no longer exists and we reign supreme!"

In the state of wisdom I had attained I was able to understand the inevitable effects of what had taken place throughout the full extent of the dimension we call time. With a voice that resounded with the prophetic sorrow of the ages, I stated sadly:

"Unto you, my companions who have wantonly chosen to deny your Source and misuse the power that He shared with you, wandering in illusory nightmares will be your fate, never having knowledge and never knowing truth from falsity. Always will it seem that the hatred is without, when in truth it is within your own mind. Thus will you dwell in a spectre of chaotic hatred, confounded in a bottomless pit of perdition, until you can change your minds.

"And to you my companions who have chosen to reject the advice of the Light beings and to continue with your madness, you will experience unending conflict, pain, sorrow and loss. Only when you can accept that you were wrong and see that the darkness and separation are within will your arrogance disappear. When you can at last let go of your self-proclaimed role of righteousness as God's first lieutenants, you will be freed from your aimless wanderings in this non-reality you call the world."

V—THE TRAP OF UNWORTHINESS

I loved both groups, and could see clearly the insanity that had occurred as I, along with my companions who had also left the middle group, proceeded towards the Light beings. We were free at last! Like a magnetic attraction, we were drawn closer and closer to the Light group. These great Light Beings held out their arms in love for us to join them, and the resplendence of this Love stirred the memory of the resplendence of our Source. Great happiness and joy engulfed us, and we stretched out our arms so that we might more quickly reach their embrace.

Suddenly out of nowhere great waves of unworthiness overcame me. I could not understand it. My self-hatred for what I believed I had done welled up and made it impossible for me to accept the Love I believed I had forsaken and forsworn. The greater the Light group's Love I allowed myself to feel, that much greater was my self-contempt: If only I had not had that passing thought—"That seems interesting; I wonder what that would be like?"; if only I had not lost that perfect awareness of who I was; if only I had not allowed my mind to wander in the vast wilderness of sleep and ignorance, guilt and judgment. If only, if only, if only—my self-recriminations would not cease.

Dissociating myself from the Light group by this guilt, I now experienced myself as a non-being, alienated from all three groups. I was in excruciating pain again and it was unbearable. In desperation I thought to myself: "Where did this come from? Who is responsible?" And I immediately looked for someone to blame. I whirled around and once again beheld in horror the physical universe, the product of that great con-

37

flict I could no longer see in myself. I turned back to the Light group and cried out:

"For your information, behold this state of darkness and iniquity that so many are confounded and trapped in."

I was lost. It was as if a bolt of lightning catapulted my awareness away from the Light group. At that very moment my mind beheld the horror that I still accused myself of being party to. As I looked down at the battleground of the world below from this mind state, out of time, there was an urgent feeling within me that I had to atone and make reparation for the devastation that I had felt responsible for. But how could I do that in this amorphous form that could only view the world-drama from an aspect in my mind above the temporal-spatial scene? Thus I made the decision that I would go to any lengths, regardless of the suffering and sacrifice entailed, to enter into this dream in all its manifold sequences to bring the message of what I had learned from sad experience. I would awaken my brother and sister components to the memory of that insane thought of separation and opposition which they had now blotted out. In doing this I assumed that I would be able to keep intact an even more ancient memory of that pristine state that once had been, before the mad idea gave birth to this vast miasma.

The decision being made, my opaque thought-form descended into all the dimensions of the nightmare dream, as if a part of me shattered into thousands of pieces, accompanied by a tremendous shock, as if an electric bolt had exploded and ripped through my very being. The pain was excruciating until oblivion overcame me. From another region of my mind I was able to understand that these thousands of pieces that were enveloped in that nightmare dream were images I had made of myself. They seemed to represent a serial drama of multiple incarnations—different aspects of my reactions of horror, pain, guilt and fear—but which had actually occurred simultaneously in an instant.

All the body-forms in which I would express my self-hatred now became clear. The dominant theme was always some form of body-identification, a body that was victim of the world and those within it—either those who sought to damn it, or those, like myself, who sought to save it. I realized the reason for this: In a world of duality, subject and object, self-hatred must have an object onto which it can project itself so it need not confront the pain of its own guilt. This projection of self-hatred, masquerading as innocence, was the path of redemption I had chosen as substitute for the true redemption the Light group held out to me. What was particularly painful for me was knowing that what I was observing was already over. Yet I was consumed by a strange belief that the road to reintegration and wholeness lay in allowing my mind, from on high, systematically to reexperience each painful event of that ongoing saga of suffering—in myself and others. It was as if through such a sacrificial process I would, one by one, bring together into wholeness all the fragmented images I had made of myself.

VI—THE RETURN HOME

Despite this involvement in the world I was aware, sometimes dimly, sometimes clearly, that a light in the form of a Voice had remained with me in some region of my mind. It was the Voice of the Holy Spirit that always comforted and assured me that what seemed to be occurring had not really occurred at all; in fact, the seeming separation was *already* over. At those times, the Holy Spirit was like a soothing balm that quieted the pain in my mind. Over seeming aeons, that sweet, loving Voice continued to call to me, patiently informing me that there was a better way of reintegration than the path I had chosen. This Voice of Wisdom said:

"My dearest child, there is no need to atone for your guilt by inflicting such pain upon yourself. Accept the idea into your most holy mind that all you are perceiving is an illusion that is over and finished, and has been undone through our loving Source. Let me shine away these serial nightmare dreams, and awaken once again the memory of our loving Creator whom you have never left. You still remain as He created you, a perfect Thought and loving extension of Himself. Forget these brutal dreams of unworthiness and accept the truth that you have been forgiven all your mistaken beliefs which have never truly occurred. Our path back to the memory of God is the undoing of your belief in the value of your method of reintegration. *You must release all judgment of yourself and others, forgiving what you still perceive as substitute for Reality.* Give over to me the decision you had made before entering the dream."

I knew exactly what the Holy Spirit was referring to. It was a decision I had made that I would go to any lengths, regardless of the suffering entailed, to enter into this dream. . . . *That* is what I had to let go. Instead of doing it my way, I had to allow the Holy Spirit to replace my nightmares with His happy dreams. Almost as if I had changed a cassette in a tape recorder in my mind, I was able finally to let the Holy Spirit decide for me. The voice of hurt and judgment faded, and in its place was the Voice of Heaven and its message of a different vision.

I now know that Help is within me, and if at any time I am tempted to react to anyone or anything in this dream as if it were real, I can call on the Help of Heaven instantly. Looking at the world, I can smile at the silly unreality of what I beheld as the substitute for Heaven. I have remembered my Source and who I am, and know that everything else, coming from my unworthiness and self-hatred, was but my own weird imaginings of a separation from God that could never be.

I share my experiences with you, my friends, so that you can avoid the mind's mistaken and illusory beliefs that gave rise to a world we apprehend through our consciousness. To believe in any portion of the world, to give credence to one single thought that the world upholds, or to fight against it, is to become trapped, singing the dirge of homage to this false system of thinking we call the ego. It is to become ensnared in an ignorance so all-encompassing that we can only liken it to a state of total oblivion and non-being. It does not feel nor appear this way, but that is the effect of the hypnotism, the hallucination within this nightmare dream that we have made to take the place of Heaven.

Above all, never forget that our loving Source has provided His holy Voice within our mind to comfort us in all seeming tribulation, to awaken us from this dream, and lead us gently back to the Home we never truly left.

Chapter 2

THE STATE OF HEAVEN

Mystics throughout the centuries have spoken of the ineffability of God and the state of Heaven. Likewise, the Course does not usually attempt to describe what is beyond description. It states that "words are but symbols of symbols. They are thus twice removed from reality" (manual, p. 51). Therefore, it is very difficult to capture the essence of this Reality of God in words that are "twice removed" from it:

> Oneness is simply the idea God is. And in His Being, He encompasses all things. No mind holds anything but Him. We say "God is," and then we cease to speak, for in that knowledge words are meaningless (workbook, p. 315).

Nonetheless, we shall at least attempt some descriptions of God and Heaven, illustrating the basic characteristics of the state of Heaven. These include: the nature of God, the process of creation, and the perfect unity of Creator and created that can never be changed or destroyed.

We begin with this beautiful and evocative passage from the Course, which asks us to reach back to the memory of that pristine stillness we believe we have lost:

> Listen,—perhaps you catch a hint of an ancient state not quite forgotten; dim, perhaps, and yet not altogether unfamiliar, like a song whose name is long forgotten, and the circumstances in which you heard completely unremembered. Not the whole song has stayed with you, but just a little wisp of melody, at-

tached not to a person or a place or anything particu-
lar. But you remember, from just this little part, how
lovely was the song, how wonderful the setting where
you heard it, and how you loved those who were there
and listened with you. . . .

Beyond the body, beyond the sun and stars, past
everything you see and yet somehow familiar, is an arc
of golden light that stretches as you look into a great
and shining circle. And all the circle fills with light
before your eyes. The edges of the circle disappear, and
what is in it is no longer contained at all. The light
expands and covers everything, extending to infinity
forever shining and with no break or limit anywhere.
Within it everything is joined in perfect continuity.
Nor is it possible to imagine that anything could be
outside, for there is nowhere that this light is not.

This is the vision of the Son of God, whom you
know well. Here is the sight of him who knows his
Father. Here is the memory of what you are; a part of
this, with all of it within, and joined to all as surely
as all is joined in you (text, pp. 416f).

God, being First Cause, is the Creator and
Source of all life. He is perfect love, eternal unity, limitless, formless and changeless. Although God obviously
is not a body, neither male nor female, in this book we
adopt the traditional Judaeo-Christian language used
by the Course. The Course's utilization of this conven-
tion is consistent with its purpose of correcting what it
views as Christianity's errors, within the context of
Christianity's conceptual language. Thus, it retains
the traditional terminology, but radically reinterprets
it.

The essence of Heaven is spirit, which "is the
Thought of God which He created like Himself. The

43

unified spirit is God's one Son, or Christ" (manual, p. 75). We find here another example of how the Course utilizes Christian terminology, but with a meaning that is entirely different from traditional usage. The traditional Christian identification of Jesus as the only Son of God, and everyone else as adopted sons, is here corrected by the Course to include all people (in fact, all "living things") as Christ. Jesus states that he is simply an "elder brother"—part of the Sonship of Christ—who is different from us in time but equal in eternity. As he says in the Course:

> *There is nothing about me that you cannot attain. I have nothing that does not come from God. The difference between us now is that I have nothing else. This leaves me in a state which is only potential in you* (text, p. 5).

Another characteristic of spirit is that it is continually extending itself, a synonym for creation. This process, however, should not be understood as having spatial dimensions, as our usage of "extend" would connote. Spirit is extended through the Mind of God, which is defined as being spirit's "activating agent . . . supplying its creative energy" (manual, p. 75).

Since God created Christ by extending Himself, and Christ shares in the attributes of His Creator, the Son must create like His Father. Thus the Course teaches that Christ is co-creator with God. God created Christ, while Christ created what the Course calls creations:

> *God, Who encompasses all being, created beings who have everything individually, but who want to share it to increase their joy. Nothing real can be increased except by sharing. That is why God created*

you. Divine Abstraction takes joy in sharing. That is
what creation means (text, p. 64).
Being must *be extended. That is how it retains the*
knowledge of itself. Spirit yearns to share its being, as
its Creator did. Created by sharing, its will is to
create. It does not wish to contain God, but wills to
extend His Being.

> *The extension of God's Being is spirit's only func-*
> *tion. Its fullness cannot be contained, any more than*
> *can the fullness of its Creator. Fullness is extension*
(text, pp. 122f).

In the language of the Course, we may say that
God is the First Person of the Trinity, while Christ and
His creations constitute the Second Person. To speak of
Christ as co-creating with God is not to say that Christ
is God: God created Christ; Christ did not create God.
This unity of God, Christ, and Christ's creations is
what the Course calls Reality.

The Course paradoxically speaks of the one Son
of God, at the same time it refers to the Sons or the
Sonship, as we see in the following quotation:

> *It should especially be noted that God has only one*
> *Son. If all His creations are His Sons, every one must*
> *be an integral part of the whole Sonship. The Sonship*
> *in its oneness transcends the sum of its parts* (text, p.
> 29).

In our myth, we used the word "Idea" to refer to
the Son of God, the unified Christ, while "Thoughts"
denoted the Sons whose Totality comprised the Sonship. The Course states:

> *Creation is the sum of all God's Thoughts, in*
> *number infinite, and everywhere without all limit.*
> *Only Love creates, and only like Itself. There was no*
> *time when all that It created was not there. Nor will*

*there be a time when anything that It created suffers
any loss. Forever and forever are God's Thoughts exactly as they were and as they are, unchanged through
time and after time is done.*

*God's Thoughts are given all the power that their
own Creator has. For He would add to Love by its
extension. Thus His Son shares in creation, and must
therefore share in power to create. . . . Creation is the
holy Son of God, for in creation is His Will complete
in every aspect, making every part container of the
Whole. Its oneness is forever guaranteed inviolate;
forever held within His holy Will, beyond all possibility of harm, of separation, imperfection and of any
spot upon its sinlessness* (workbook, p. 451).

Creation is perfectly changeless and perfectly unified:

*The changelessness of Heaven is in you. . . . The
still infinity of endless peace surrounds you gently in
its soft embrace, so strong and quiet, tranquil in the
might of its Creator, nothing can intrude upon the
sacred Son of God within* (text, p. 570).

*Heaven is not a place nor a condition. It is merely
an awareness of perfect oneness, and the knowledge
that there is nothing else; nothing outside this oneness,
and nothing else within* (text, 359).

The word "knowledge" is used by the Course to
denote the non-dualistic state of Heaven, and is independent of the popular usage that implies the duality of
subject and object, the knower and what is known.
The Course also states:

*In Heaven is everything God values, and nothing else.
Heaven is perfectly unambiguous. Everything is clear
and bright, and calls forth one response. There is no
darkness and there is no contrast. There is no varia-*

tion. *There is no interruption. There is a sense of peace so deep that no dream in this world has ever brought even a dim imagining of what it is* (text, pp. 248f).

The immutability of God and His Son, forever one, is a reflection of this important principle of the Course: Ideas leave not their source. We are Thoughts (Ideas) in the Mind of God, and therefore can never leave our Source, the Mind that created us. It is this truth that corrects our misbelief in the separation, and thus expresses the principle of the Atonement. The centrality of this teaching is highlighted by the fact that, in the form of the statement "I am as God created me," it is used as the title of three workbook lessons, not to mention its frequent expression throughout the entire Course:

> *Christ is God's Son as He created Him. He is the Self we share, uniting us with one another, and with God as well. He is the Thought Which still abides within the Mind that is His Source. He has not left His holy home, nor lost the innocence in which He was created. He abides unchanged forever in the Mind of God* (workbook, p. 421).

> *Nothing that God knows not exists. And what He knows exists forever, changelessly. For thoughts endure as long as does the mind that thought of them. And in the Mind of God there is no ending, nor a time in which His Thoughts were absent or could suffer change . . . And so there are no separate parts in what exists within God's Mind. It is forever one, eternally united and at peace* (text, p. 587).

Created by Love, in Love, we as Christ are Love. As Thoughts in the Mind of Love, we can never leave this Source. Without beginning and without end, this

Love that is Christ flows unceasingly from Itself to Its Source, and from Its Source to Itself. Thus, there is no place where God the Father ends and Christ the Son begins. We are forever an Effect, joined with Him Who is our Cause.

Chapter 3

DESCENT INTO HELL:
THE SEPARATION FROM GOD

The Course states:
Into eternity, where all is one, there crept a tiny, mad idea, at which the Son of God remembered not to laugh. In his forgetting did the thought become a serious idea, and possible of both accomplishment and real effects (text, p. 544).

The "tiny, mad idea" is expressed in our myth by one component of the Sonship suddenly having the thought: "Can there be an opposite to what is?" In other words, "Is this all there is; can there be other than what is; something else?" The exact words of course do not matter, but their meaning and implication most certainly do.

The very concept of an opposite to Reality that is expressed in the above thought—"Can there be an opposite to what is?"—is really a statement concealed in question form. Because the state of Heaven is Everything, the very question itself, by considering the possibility of there being "something else," already implies the dualistic notion that there can be an opposite to Heaven that can be supplied by this "something else." By introducing this duality the Oneness and Abundance of our Source are denied. Since God established Reality as total unity, the belief in dualism inherently dismisses Reality and substitutes a perversion of truth at best, and a hell at worst. As the Course states:

For this world is the opposite of Heaven, being made to be its opposite, and everything takes a direction exactly opposite of what is true. In Heaven, where the meaning of love is known, love is the same as union. Here, where the illusion of love is accepted in love's place, love is perceived as separation and exclusion (text, p. 317).

The seeming result of that "tiny, mad idea," therefore, was casting ourselves out of Heaven and disinheriting ourselves from our Creator. A part of God, believing it could cut itself off from its Source, rendered itself Sourceless, not to mention depriving the Source of Its Effects (Christ). The Course comments:

Earlier, we spoke of your desire to create your own Creator, and be father and not son to Him. . . . The Son is the effect, whose Cause he would deny. And so he seems to be the cause, producing real effects (text, p. 420).

In the context of magic thoughts, in which the Course includes all our post-separation ego thoughts, the impossible now seemed possible:

A magic thought, by its mere presence, acknowledges a separation from God. It states, in the clearest form possible, that the mind which believes it has a separate will that can oppose the Will of God, also believes it can succeed. That this can hardly be a fact is obvious. Yet that it can be believed as fact is equally obvious. And herein lies the birthplace of guilt (manual, p. 43).

Thus, by placing the idea of separation within the context of magic thoughts, the Course teaches that the separation is illusory, not to mention inconceivable: A part of God (the Sonship) and His Will cannot have a separate will that opposes what is itself. As the Course states:

50

*All that the ego is, is an idea that it is possible that
things should happen to the Son of God without his
will; and thus without the Will of his Creator,
Whose Will cannot be separate from his own. This is
the Son of God's replacement for his will, a mad
revolt against what must forever be. This is the statement that he has the power to make God powerless
and so to take it for himself, and leave himself without
what God has willed for him. This is the mad idea
you have enshrined upon your altars, and which you
worship* (text, p. 419).

Moreover, God does not even know what has happened:

*Spirit in its knowledge is unaware of the ego. It does
not attack; it merely cannot conceive of it at all* (text,
p. 53).

Yet, this does not prevent our *believing* in what is inconceivable:

*Everyone is free to refuse to accept his inheritance, but
he is not free to establish what his inheritance is*
(text, p. 44).

Because the Son of God is a unity, the single
thought of separation that is described in the myth laser beamed through the entire Sonship. It was as if a
part of the collective Sonship lifted off as a layer of
cellophane, catapulting itself into a void of nowhere.
The Course refers to this as the "detour into fear,"
involving a four step process:

*First, you believe that what God created can be
changed by your own mind.*

*Second, you believe that what is perfect can be ren-
dered imperfect or lacking.*

*Third, you believe that you can distort the creations
of God, including yourself.*

51

Fourth, you believe that you can create yourself, and that the direction of your own creation is up to you.

These related distortions represent a picture of what actually occurred in the separation or the "detour into fear." None of this existed before the separation, nor does it actually exist now (text, p. 14).

If the separation is only a bad dream and does not exist, it is natural to wonder why we experience it as if it were real.

How can you who are God's meaning perceive yourself as absent from it? You can see yourself as separated from your meaning only by experiencing yourself as unreal (text, p. 108).

Existence, as defined by the Course, is a false or illusory substitute for the Divine Abstraction of Being. Since our minds are very powerful, we believe we can invert, subvert and change reality, as noted above in the "detour into fear," into a "something else" that seems to be apart from the truth of Heaven. In other words, we have denied our true Identity as Christ and assumed a false identity as an ego.

The whole matter boils down to the Authority problem which, the Course says, is the "root of all evil." We believe that we have authored our own existence by usurping the power of God and establishing our own self-creation.

. . . but you prefer to be anonymous when you choose to separate yourself from your Author. Being uncertain of your true Authorship, you believe that your creation was anonymous. This leaves you in a position where it sounds meaningful to believe that you created yourself. The dispute over Authorship has left such uncertainty in your mind that it may even doubt whether you really exist at all (text, p. 43).

The ego is the thought of separation given form. It is the belief that we have created ourselves and destroyed our true Creator. This is succinctly explained by the following passage:

The ego is idolatry; the sign of limited and separated self, born in a body, doomed to suffer and to end its life in death. It is the "will" that sees the Will of God as enemy, and takes a form in which it is denied. The ego is the "proof" that strength is weak and love is fearful, life is really death, and what opposes God alone is true.

The ego is insane. In fear it stands beyond the Everywhere, apart from All, in separation from the Infinite. In its insanity it thinks it has become a victor over God Himself. And in its terrible autonomy it "sees" the Will of God has been destroyed (workbook, p. 457).

Moreover, the issue is not so much the thought of separation (the ego) that laser beamed through the Sonship, but the reactions to that thought. These reactions are the basic focus of the Course. In the myth we spoke of three separate groups and their respective responses to this thought. However, in reflecting on our individual experiences here it is best to consider that each of us, walking this world as seemingly separate Sons, contains within ourselves aspects of all three groups: the dark group, where the original thought of separation arose; the Light group, who did not take the thought of separation seriously and therefore did not oppose it; and the middle group, somehow caught between the two, who took the thought of separation very seriously and thus wanted to defend God from the attack of the dark group, seeking its defeat. We shall now describe some psychological aspects of the three groups.

The singleminded purpose of the dark group was to usurp God's Authorship, and in so doing defeat God and enthrone themselves in His place. They knew they could not do this in the state of Reality, but by leaving Heaven their wishes could be accomplished. Since "all beliefs are real to the believer" (text, p. 45), the dark group believed that they had wrested power from their Creator. The Course describes the situation in many different places, for example:

> The mind can make the belief in separation very real and very fearful, and this belief is the "devil." It is powerful, active, destructive and clearly in opposition to God, because it literally denies His Fatherhood. . . . (text, p. 45)

> The "devil" is a frightening concept because he seems to be extremely powerful and extremely active. He is perceived as a force in combat with God, battling Him for possession of His creations (text, p. 44f).

Digressing slightly, we have chosen these particular passages because of the Christian understanding of the role of the devil. According to traditional theology, the devil is seen as an outside agent who tempts humans through deception and is thus responsible for the wrong choices people make. Psychologically this belief is quite understandable for it affords us the easy way out, allowing us to avoid responsibility for our own thoughts and decisions. However, this makes no real sense for it denies the power of our mind to choose. Since we had chosen the separation in the beginning we must be free to choose differently now.

In conclusion, we can see that the dark group represents the part of our separated mind that consistently chooses to deny, attack and murder God, substituting fear for love, and striving to establish an opposite to Heaven. It is what the Course calls the ego (or the "wrong mind") and, in this powerful passage, it is equated with the anti-Christ, another example of the Course's redefinition of a traditional Christian term:

This is the anti-Christ; the strange idea there is a power past omnipotence, a place beyond the infinite, a time transcending the eternal. Here the world of idols has been set by the idea this power and place and time are given form, and shape the world where the impossible has happened. Here the deathless come to die, the all-encompassing to suffer loss, the timeless to be made the slaves of time. Here does the changeless change; the peace of God, forever given to all living things, give way to chaos. And the Son of God, as perfect, sinless and as loving as his Father, come to hate a little while; to suffer pain and finally to die (text, p. 576).

The Light group, on the opposite end of the spectrum, did not identify with this thought of separation, and retained within itself the awareness of Who it is (the Christ) and the perfect memory of its Creator. The part of our mind (the "right mind") that reflects the Light group is the home of the Holy Spirit, Who is defined in the Course as the Voice for God, the Answer to our question (Can there be an opposite to what is?). He is also described as "the communication link between God the Father and His separated Sons" (text, p. 88). Created by God to awaken His sleeping Son from his nightmare dreams, the Holy Spirit's function is to enter into the dream and comfort the Son, calling to him to "awaken and be glad." Thus He is also referred to as the Comforter.

The Course metaphorically describes God's thought after the separation: "My children sleep and must be awakened." And then comments:

How can you wake children in a more kindly way than by a gentle Voice That will not frighten them, but will merely remind them that the night is over and the light has come? (text, p. 96)

It is the Holy Spirit who reminds the Son "to laugh" at the original thought of separation. In other words, we are counselled not to take it seriously because the separation could not happen in Reality, but only in insanity.

The middle group is the home of conflict and fear because it accords reality to both the Light and dark groups, and cannot really distinguish between truth and illusion. It was as if when that thought of separation laser beamed throughout the Sonship those that gravitated to the middle group experienced themselves contaminated by a virulent virus. One might imagine them remarking to themselves at that original thought, "That is interesting, I wonder what that might be like?" In that instant they laid the seeds for making that thought real in their minds, and thus "possible of both accomplishment and real effects." Their original guilt lies here, for because of their having entertained that thought of separation, even if only for an instant, they believed contamination had infected them. This contamination is what the Course refers to as sin, of which guilt is the psychological experience, and fear its inevitable end product.

The dream state known as the separation is actually a nightmare, whose principal components are the unholy trinity of sin, guilt and fear: *Sin* represents the belief that we could indeed separate ourselves from

God and usurp His place as First Cause and Prime Creator. The childhood game of King of the Mountain is reminiscent of our sin, wherein children continually vie to be the sole possessor of the area on top of a mound of soil. It is our identification with the ego self that leads us to believe that our dream has become reality. *Guilt* upholds this belief and, moreover, carries with it the recrimination that we have done a terrible thing to our Father and Source by attacking and opposing His Will. Because of this guilt we inevitably believe that God must seek to avenge Himself by punishing us for the place we stole from Him. We cannot help, therefore, but *fear* this retaliatory wrath from Heaven. Thus we can say that our nightmare dream of sin, guilt and fear has become a battlefield, in which God and His Sons have become enemies. The Course summarizes this situation:

> *Think what this seems to do to the relationship between the Father and the Son. Now it appears that they can never be one again. For one must always be condemned, and by the other. Now are they different, and enemies. And their relationship is one of opposition . , . And fear of God and of each other now appears as sensible, made real by what the Son of God has done both to himself and his Creator* (text, p. 456).

Referring to the chart in the Appendix, the top right-hand side represents the dream in which part of the Son's Mind has seemingly separated (the dotted line) from Itself, the Christ Mind. This split mind is the ego and consciousness, and represents the false self we believe we are within the dream. As the Course states:

> *Consciousness, the level of perception, was the first*

*split introduced into the mind after the separation,
making the mind a perceiver rather than a creator.
Consciousness is correctly identified as the domain of
the ego. The ego is a wrong-minded attempt to perceive yourself as you wish to be, rather than as you are*
(text, p. 37).

Not being able to exist in such a state of intense
horror and fear, the split mind, now individualized,
represses and denies the entire thought of separation
and any responsibility for it. Rather than confronting
the "sin" it has believed exists within itself, and letting
itself feel the unreality of the terror of God's wrath, it
perverts the mind's process of extension into what the
Course terms "projection." What has been perceived
and made real within, is now perceived and made real
without. As the Course states:

> *Projection makes perception. . . . It [what we
> perceive] is the witness to your state of mind, the out-
> side picture of an inward condition* (text, p. 415).

Here we can fully understand why each
component-Son of the middle group, experiencing
such guilt and fear, drove itself to project the responsibility for the separation onto the dark group, seeing in
it what it judged to be the evil sin within. Thus, it
believed that it was different and separate from the
other component-Sons. This also accounts for the middle group's lack of understanding of the message of the
Light group. Its experience of loss of the Kingdom,
and attendant feelings of bewilderment and fear of the
chaotic void it now found itself in, rendered it devoid of
clarity. As the horror of these feelings engulfed the middle group they had to blame someone for the painfully
inconsolable situation in which they found themselves.
The dark group met this need nicely, and so they be-

came the scapegoats onto whose head full responsibility for the separation was placed.

The Course urges us:

> Forget not that the witness to the world of evil cannot speak except for what has seen a need for evil in the world. And this is where your guilt was first beheld. In separation from your brother was the first attack upon yourself begun. . . . This is how all illusions came about. The one who makes them does not see himself as making them, and their reality does not depend on him. Whatever cause they have is something quite apart from him, and what he sees is separate from his mind. He cannot doubt his dreams' reality, because he does not see the part he plays in making them and making them seem real (text, pp. 540f).

Chapter 4

THE MAKING OF THE WORLD: A HIDING PLACE

Twentieth century science has made great progress in its study of the origin and nature of the physical universe. In fact, some cosmologists believe that they can trace its entire evolutionary progression—spanning billions of years—*except* for the initial split seconds that preceded the Big Bang that gave rise to the world. The following is an attempt to describe what preceded and followed that instant.

In the discussion of our myth we left off with the middle group's projection of its guilt onto the dark group, thereby holding them responsible for what it experienced as the monstrous effects of the thought of separation. This need to project blame caused the middle group to oppose the designs of the dark group's experiment in the making of a world that would be the substitute for Heaven.

This need also prevented the middle group from understanding the message of non-opposition that the Holy Spirit, the Voice of the Light group, was trying to teach them. Thus, the middle group found itself in the paradoxical situation of opposing both groups, intensifying the experience of separation. Compounding this incredible dilemma still further, the middle group blotted out of awareness the guilt of having betrayed God a second time: first, by entertaining for a split second that thought of separation, framed in the hypothetical question: "That is interesting, I wonder what that might be like?"; secondly, by taking upon themselves the defense of God and His Kingdom by initiating a great crusade to oppose and stop the dark group, whom they considered to be the evil ones. They denied their own reponsibility in experiencing the effects of that unreal thought of separation, and so did not recognize or realize that God's message through the Holy Spirit is: "Love does not oppose; do not make the error real." Thus, they in effect turned their back on God a second time.

Now, unfortunately, the battle lines became drawn, and in the middle group's opposition to the dark group's *thought* of opposition the error was made real with the resultant emergence of the phenomenal universe. The following passage in the Course is reminiscent of the advice the Light group would have given to these declarations of war; advice, however, which continued to go unheeded:

> Every response to the ego is a call to war, and war does deprive you of peace. Yet in this war there is no opponent. This is the reinterpretation of reality that you must make to secure peace, and the only one you need ever make. Those whom you perceive as opponents are part of your peace, which you are giving up by attacking them. How can you have what you give up? (text, p. 128)

As we have already seen in the myth, the middle group wanted no part of the Light group's peace, and instead countered the dark group's outward projection of thought by emitting what *they believed* was a pure thought of light, not realizing that they had been contaminated by the very thought of duality and separation in themselves. It was as if the middle group tried to cure the dark group's infection with infected hands. That is why the Course states: "Trust not your good intentions. They are not enough" (text, p. 355).

The unclarity of their thinking, as we have just seen, was induced by their denial of any participation in the separation and responsibility for it. The situation was further compounded by their need to deny any guilt in themselves, and therefore the need to project it onto the dark group. Hence the first round of battle between the middle and dark groups produced the Big Bang and the formation of the cosmos.

If the middle group could have stopped at this point to contemplate the meaning of what they beheld, they would not have become further entrapped in antagonism, conflict and opposition. They would have simply stepped back, "shaken the dust from their feet," and "crossed over" to the Light group. However, as we have seen, the attraction to that opposition was very intense, and precluded their hearing the Voice of Sanity.

Reason would have shown the middle group that had they not opposed what they perceived to be the intentions of the dark group (which were also *their* thoughts, yet heavily denied), the material universe would never have come into existence. It was the very opposition to the thought of making a substitute for Heaven that solidified that thought and gave it its seeming reality. Without that opposition, the dark group's thought would have remained isolated and without effect. It took both the dark *and* middle groups to make the world, as both had agreed that the error of separation was real. At that point it did become, *for them*, "possible of both accomplishment and real effects."

The second, third and fourth rounds of battle began in a point-counterpoint rhythm, fashioning the mineral, vegetable and animal kingdoms. As we have seen in the myth, the last and greatest projection produced a creature that would have "dominion over . . . all the earth" (Genesis 2:26). Here the rhythm changed, with the middle group emitting the thought first, having the need to wrest from the dark group the control over what had already been made. That is why the middle group is so attached to, identified with, and protective of the human scene and the body. In fact, the body becomes a major way we are caught up in this world, as we shall see below.

Thus we observe that the thoughts of separation —fear, hatred and attack—solidified into the form we call matter, and gave rise to a world of fear, hatred and attack. This world clearly was the opposite of the Kingdom of God, whose resplendent glory had to be denied by the middle group if the illusory nature of its actions were to be maintained. The Course asks us, as the Light group asked the middle group:

> Consider the kingdom you have made and judge its worth fairly. Is it worthy to be a home for a child of God? Does it protect his peace and shine love upon him? Does it keep his heart untouched by fear, and allow him to give always, without any sense of loss? Does it teach him that this giving is his joy, and that God Himself thanks him for his giving? This is the only environment in which you can be happy. You cannot make it, any more than you can make yourself. It has been created for you, as you were created for it. God watches over His children and denies them nothing. Yet when they deny Him they do not know this, because they denied themselves everything. You who

63

could give the Love of God to everything you see and touch and remember, are literally denying Heaven to yourself (text, p. 126).

In the post-separation state, as the Course teaches, "All thinking produces form at some level" (text, p. 27), since that was the intent of the separation thought itself. Therefore, it should come as no surprise that the formlessness of Heaven was rendered into form. Furthermore, the content of the formlessness of Heaven is love, whereas the content of form is fear, hatred, attack and opposition, being all the qualities of the post-separation state. Succinctly stated, the Course teaches that "The world was made as an attack on God" (workbook, p. 403), and it means this very literally. This is a fact that, except for the Light group, has been blotted out of awareness. We see this especially in the middle group that has taken on for itself the role of defender of the truth.

We may well wonder why the Course states that the world was made as an attack on God. If Love is our Reality, wanting to be separate from that Love is not only a denial of who we are, but an attack on Love itself. Since Love is of God and is the state of the Kingdom, the separation must also be an attack on Him. Our identification and investment in the world we have made has obscured our objectivity on this issue, and prevented us from discerning the true origin of this phenomenal universe. Throughout the ages we have cleverly skirted this issue by imputing to God the making of this world in an attempt to delude ourselves, projecting onto Him the responsibility for its origin and nature. Remember that the original intention of the dark group was to "make the infinite finite, the limitless limited, and the abstract concrete and spe-

64

cific." This is most clearly an attack, subsequently reinforced by the middle group's opposition. The Course provides a powerful description of what happened in the separation:

> You who believe that God is fear made but one substitution. It has taken many forms, because it was the substitution of illusion for truth; of fragmentation for wholeness. It has become so splintered and subdivided and divided again, over and over, that it is now almost impossible to perceive it once was one, and still is what it was. That one error, which brought truth to illusion infinity to time, and life to death, was all you ever made. Your whole world rests upon it. Everything you see reflects it, and every special relationship that you have ever made is part of it.
>
> You may be surprised to hear how very different is reality from what you see. You do not realize the magnitude of that one error. It was so vast and so completely incredible that from it a world of total unreality had to emerge. What else could come of it? Its fragmented aspects are fearful enough, as you begin to look at them. But nothing you have seen begins to show you the enormity of the original error, which seemed to cast you out of Heaven, to shatter knowledge into meaningless bits of disunited perceptions, and to force you to make further substitutions.
>
> That was the first projection of error outward

(text, pp. 347f).

Thus far we have only spoken about the making of space by the error of projecting the thought of separation outward. Time is an equally important ingredient in the ego's plan against God and, in fact, is really no different, as stated in the following passage:

> For time and space are one illusion [separation],

65

*which takes different forms. If it has been projected
beyond your mind you think of it as time. The nearer
it is brought to where it is, the more you think of it in
terms of space* (text, p. 519).

Just as the seemingly infinite nature of the physical universe was made to replicate the true infinity of Heaven, so too was the seemingly endless span of evolutionary time established to replicate eternity. However, when one compares the spatial-temporal world we have made with the true resplendence of the infinite and eternal—God and Christ—one can only see in the ego's miscreation a cruel parody and mocking travesty of truth.

Moreover, the belief in the reality of time also became the ego's perfect defense against the fact that time is finished. The Course emphasizes, as we shall see presently, that in the same instant that the thought of separation occurred, in that same instant God created the Holy Spirit and *the error was corrected and undone.* Time was thus over in the same instant that it seemed to begin. As the Course explains:

> *To you who still believe you live in time and know
> not it is gone, the Holy Spirit still guides you through
> the infinitely small and senseless maze you still per-
> ceive in time, though it has long since gone. You think
> you live in what is past. Each thing you look upon
> you saw but for an instant, long ago, before its unre-
> ality gave way to truth. Not one illusion still remains
> unanswered in your mind. Uncertainty was brought
> to certainty so long ago that it is hard indeed to hold it
> to your heart, as if it were before you still.*
>
> *The tiny instant you would keep and make eternal,
> passed away in Heaven to soon for anything to notice
> it had come. What disappeared too quickly to affect*

*the simple knowledge of the Son of God can hardly
still be there, for you to choose to be your teacher. Only
in the past,—an ancient past, too short to make a
world in answer to creation,—did this world appear
to rise. So very long ago, for such a tiny interval of
time, that not one note in Heaven's song was missed*
(text, pp. 511f).

Here, as probably in no other part of the ego's
system, we see the power of the world's insanity in
preserving a dimension of experience that is past and
gone. The past, present and future are nothing but the
seemingly endless replay of that ancient instant, *which
is already over.*

> *Yet in each unforgiving act or thought, in every
> judgment and in all belief in sin, is that one instant
> still called back, as if it could be made again in time.
> You keep an ancient memory before your eyes. . . .*
>
> *Each day, and every minute in each day, and every
> instant that each minute holds, you but relive the sin-
> gle instant when the time of terror took the place of
> love. And so you die each day to live again, until you
> cross the gap between the past and present, which is
> not a gap at all. Such is each life; a seeming interval
> from birth to death and on to life again, a repetition of
> an instant gone by long ago that cannot be relived.
> And all of time is but the mad belief that what is over
> is still here and now* (text, pp. 512f).

While the Course itself does not take a definitive
position on the question of reincarnation—the point
being that multiple illusory births are the same as a
single one, and salvation is only possible in the dimension of time we believe we are in—passages such as the
above seem to imply that within the illusion of time we
have chosen repeatedly to experience that terrifying in-

stant of separation until we finally choose to awaken from this recurring nightmare and leave time for eternity. Only then could we truly understand these words from the Course: "You have reached the end of an ancient journey, not realizing yet that it is over" (text, p. 366).

What rips aside the veil that would conceal the face of grim devastation is recognizing that death, as described in the Course, is "the central dream from which all illusions stem" (manual, p. 63). For what is the passage of time but the context for the inevitable loss of what we in our arrogance have called life?

Is it not madness to think of life as being born, aging, losing vitality, and dying in the end? . . . It is the one fixed, unchangeable belief of the world that all things in it are born only to die. This is regarded as "the way of nature," . . . the "natural" law of life (manual, p. 63).

What seems to be the opposite of life [death] is merely sleeping. When the mind elects to be what it is not, and to assume an alien power which it does not have, a foreign state it cannot enter, or a false condition not within its Source, it merely seems to go to sleep a while. It dreams of time; an interval in which what seems to happen never has occurred, the changes wrought are substanceless, and all events are nowhere. When the mind awakes, it but continues as it always was (workbook, p. 312).

As was stated in the myth, this destructibility of all "created things" raises the ego, in its insanity, above God who does not have the "power" to take away the life He created. How perfectly, then, does the world fulfill the ego's purpose by being the exact oposite of Heaven! Thus, whenever we make any aspect of this world real in our minds, whether it be as an object of pleasure or pain, we but reinforce the insane belief that the impossible has been accomplished, and with real effects. We would have once again made the error real, and so is our sin against our loving Source continually thrust before our eyes. The guilt over what we believe we have done screams relentlessly: "You are unworthy to be loved by God and returned to His Kingdom!" This profound sense of unworthiness thus seems forever to preclude our acceptance of the Holy Spirit's loving answer to this mad belief.

In the myth, this dynamic of guilt's power is portrayed by the speaker's inability to return to the Light group because of the strong hold the mind had on its own unworthiness. This is what *A Course in Miracles* calls the attraction of guilt, which is how the ego keeps the mind imprisoned and ensures our continuing belief in the ego's own existence.

Chapter 5

LEVEL ONE: GOD OR THE EGO

The cosmic drama that seems to pit God and the ego in an eternal struggle for supremacy reflects what we call Level One. Included on this level are all the metaphysical statements we have been considering that relate to the truth of God and His Heaven, and to the origin and nature of the illusory world. God and the ego, Heaven and the world, truth and illusion—are mutually exclusive states with no meeting place between them. The practical teachings of forgiveness, on the other hand, fall within Level Two. While the Course itself does not directly distinguish between these two levels, it nonetheless presents its message within this framework. Therefore, for the purposes of this book we shall follow this model. The chart in the Appendix presents Levels One and Two and their relationship to each other.

The Course teaches that the instant that the thought of separation occurred God gave His Answer, which is the Holy Spirit:

The instant the idea of separation entered the mind of God's Son, in that same instant was God's Answer given (manual, p. 4).

In the language of the myth, when a cellophane layer, symbolizing a part of the Sonship, lifted off and seemed to depart from Heaven it carried with it the memory of God's Love. This memory is the Holy Spirit who, as the Voice for God, remains ever present in the mind of His sleeping Son. He continually provides the answer to the ego's thought of separation, also present in the mind of the sleeping Son. As we have seen, the voice of the Light group is the Holy Spirit.

The ego hardly experiences the Holy Spirit's presence as a comfort. Rather, it perceives Him as an intrusive threat who brings the entirely different message of the Atonement to the Son's sleeping mind. This is the message that the separation never truly happened, being nothing more than an illusory dream. As the Course states, in summary of itself:

Nothing real can be threatened.
Nothing unreal exists.
Herein lies the peace of God (text, intro.).

Our only remaining choice in the post-separated belief state is between being host to God by listening to His Voice—the Holy Spirit—or being hostage to the ego. However, if the Son's sleeping mind listens to the "still, small Voice" of the Holy Spirit, it will awaken from the dream of separation and the ego will be no more:

Thoughts of God [through the Holy Spirit] are unacceptable to the ego, because they clearly point to the nonexistence of the ego itself (text, p. 59).

The ego, then, must do something to avoid what it deems to be its extinction.

Unable to defeat God's loving Voice in head-on combat, the ego is nonetheless able to nullify this loving Presence by changing It to something else. Playing upon the Son's guilt the ego convinces the sleeping Son that the Holy Spirit is the angry God's avenging messenger, hellbent on the Son's destruction. Therefore:

Atonement thus becomes a myth, and vengeance, not forgiveness, is the Will of God. From where all this begins, there is no sight of help that can succeed. Only

destruction can be the outcome. And God Himself
seems to be siding with it, to overcome His Son (text,
p. 456).

Thoroughly deluded by the ego's lies the sleeping
Son listens to the ego, which has now become his men-
tor and "savior," and seeks to flee from the Holy
Spirit. The ego urges the Son to escape from the Holy
Spirit by leaving the mind which has become the battlefield on which the Son will be destroyed. Thus the
ego has told us literally to go "out of our mind"; as the
Course frequently reminds us the entire ego system is
insane.

This "leaving the mind" is what is known psychologically as projection, wherein what was within the
mind is now seen outside of it. Remember—what was
within the split mind was the thought of separation,
now projected outward, and so what is apprehended
outside the mind is this thought given form; i.e., a separated world of matter that manifests the ego's separation. This is the Course's presentation of the making or
miscreating of the world which, as we have seen, is
analogous to the scientists' Big Bang hypothesis for the
origin of the universe.

The total physical universe is thus understood by
the Course to be a defense undertaken by the ego in an
act of defiant miscreation, to protect itself from its own
fearful image of God:

The fundamental conflict in this world, then, is be-
tween creation and miscreation. All fear is implicit in
the second, and all love in the first. The conflict is
therefore one between love and fear (text, p. 28).

The Course's explanation is clearly the antithesis
of the Judaeo-Christian view that the world is the creation of God:

The world you see is an illusion of a world. God did not create it, for what He creates must be as eternal as Himself. Yet there is nothing in the world you see that will endure forever. Some things will last in time a little while longer than others. But the time will come when all things visible will have an end (manual, p. 81).

What seems *eternal all will have an end. The stars will disappear, and night and day will be no more. All things that come and go, the tides, the seasons and the lives of men; all things that change with time and bloom and fade will not return. Where time has set an end is not where the eternal is* (text, p. 572).

To emphasize the point still further, the Course distinguishes between the spirit God *created* and the world the ego *made*:

Since the separation, the words "create" and "make" have become confused. . . . The ego is the questioning aspect of the post-separation self, which was made rather than created (text pp. 39,37).

The Holy Spirit and the ego are the only choices open to you. God created one, and so you cannot eradicate it. You made the other, and so you can. Only what God creates is irreversible and unchangeable. What you made can always be changed . . . (text, p. 78).

The Course is unequivocal on this point of God's non-creation of the physical world, and no compromise is possible here without rendering ineffectual its entire thought system. The uncompromising position the Course takes towards the integrity of its teaching is reflected in the following statement:

This course will be believed entirely or not at all. For it is wholly true or wholly false, and cannot be but partially believed. And you will either escape from

misery entirely or not at all. Reason will tell you that
there is no middle ground where you can pause uncer-
tainly, waiting to choose between the joy of Heaven
and the misery of hell. Until you choose Heaven, you
are in hell and misery (text, p. 440).

To restate the ego's rationale: Recognizing that it
could not overcome the Holy Spirit's Presence in the
mind the ego sought to conceal itself in a material
world it had to make so that it could hide. Moreover, as
part of this plan of escape from God the ego began
fragmenting itself, over and over, as it materialized itself in form, almost as if it hoped to find safety in quan-
titative fragments which would dilute the Holy Spirit's
Presence in the mind.

The biblical myth of Adam and Eve provides an
interesting parallel to the Course's version, when we
reinterpret the story with the ego as protagonist rather
than God. We quote from the Course:

> *The Garden of Eden, or the pre-separation condi-*
> *tion, was a state of mind in which nothing was*
> *needed. When Adam listened to the "lies of the ser-*
> *pent," all he heard was untruth. . . . What is seen*
> *in dreams seems to be very real. Yet the Bible says that*
> *a deep sleep fell upon Adam, and nowhere is there*
> *reference to his waking up. . . .*
>
> *All fear is ultimately reducible to the basic misper-*
> *ception that you have the ability to usurp the power of*
> *God. . . . Only after the deep sleep fell upon Adam*
> *could he experience nightmares* (text, pp. 14f).
> *God does not believe in retribution. His Mind does*
> *not create that way. . . . This kind of error is respon-*
> *sible for a host of related errors, including the belief*
> *that God rejected Adam and forced him out of the*
> *Garden of Eden* (text, pp. 32f).

74

It was not God who sought to punish Adam by expelling him from Heaven, but the willfulness of the ego that talked the sleeping Son into believing that it could be safe in a world the ego made, rather than the one God created. From its point of view, of course, the ego was correct in being threatened. But the Son does not have to listen to its voice. As the Course urges us: "You do not have to continue to believe what is not true unless you choose to do so" (text, p. 14). But we are getting ahead of our story.

Thus the material universe—in which the Course includes *all* universes,—serves the ego's purpose of concealing Reality from the Son. It is a smokescreen which also serves as a camouflage in which to hide. The ego tells us we are hiding from God; in reality the world enables us to hide from our guilt. In the continuation of the passage on the making of the world quoted in the last chapter, the Course describes this dynamic:

The world arose to hide it [the original error], and became the screen on which it [the separation] was projected and drawn between you and the truth. For truth extends inward, where the idea of loss is meaningless and only increase is conceivable. Do you really think it strange that a world in which everything is backwards and upside down [a reference to the upside-down retinal image] arose from this projection of error? For truth brought to this could only remain within in quiet, and take no part in all the mad projection by which this world was made. Call it not sin but madness, for such it was and so it still remains. Invest it not with guilt, for guilt implies it was accomplished in reality (text, p. 348).

The capstone of the ego's plan to evade the Holy Spirit is the making of the body:

The ego's fundamental wish is to replace God. In fact, the ego is the physical embodiment of that wish. For it is that wish that seems to surround the mind with a body, keeping it separate and alone, and unable to reach other minds except through the body that was made to imprison it (workbook, p. 122).

It is the body—the embodiment of the ego—that convinces the Son that the physical world is real. Yet the body was made as part of the ego's plan to conceal Reality, and so can hardly be thought to be a reliable witness. As part of a longer passage describing this role of the world and the body in "protecting" us from our guilt, the Course states:

From the world of bodies, made by insanity, insane messages seem to be returned to the mind that made it. And these messages bear witness to this world, pronouncing it as true. . . . Everything these messages relay to you is quite external. There are no messages that speak of what lies underneath [Reality], for it is not the body that could speak of this. Its eyes perceive it not; its senses remain quite unaware of it; its tongue cannot relay its messages (text, p. 367).

Consider for a moment: What is it but the body that states in no uncertain terms that the separation is indeed real? What is it but the body that witnesses that truth (spirit) being invisible does not exist, and illusions (materiality) being visible do?

When you made visible what is not true, what is true became invisible to you (text, p. 217).

What is it that tells us that there is a world out there to be seen, heard, tasted, smelled and felt? that judges what is beautiful and what is ugly? that perceives separation within and without itself? It is the body! Our sensory organs relay messages of the

76

"outer" world to our brains, which then interprets them as differing portraits of the so-called real world. And yet, as the Course states, the body is the one thing in all the world that does *not* know what Reality is:

> *The body cannot know. And while you limit your awareness to its tiny senses, you will not see the grandeur that surrounds you* (text, p. 364).

Thus all the causes, situations and events in human history, when viewed from this perspective, have been attempts by the middle group to uphold this false identification with miscreation.

> *The ability to perceive made the body possible, because you must perceive* something *and* with *something* (text, p. 38).

It is of this miscreated self ("this transient stranger") we ask for help in learning who we are:

> *Ask not this transient stranger, "What am I?" He is the only thing in all the universe that does not know. Yet it is he you ask, and it is to his answer that you would adjust. . . . To it you turn to ask the meaning of the universe. And of the one blind thing in all the seeing universe of truth you ask, "How shall I look upon the Son of God?"* (text, p. 401)

The Course later describes the insanity of this world's dream:

> *The dreaming of the world takes many forms, because the body seeks in many ways to prove it is autonomous and real. It puts things on itself that it has bought with little metal discs or paper strips the world proclaims as valuable and real. It works to get them, doing senseless things, and tosses them away for senseless things it does not need and does not even want. It hires other bodies, that they may protect it and collect more senseless things that it can call its own. It looks*

*about for special bodies that can share its dream.
Sometimes it dreams it is a conqueror of bodies weaker
than itself. But in some phases of the dream, it is the
slave of bodies that would hurt and torture it* (text,
p. 543).

*What is the world except a little gap perceived to tear
eternity apart, and break it into days and months and
years? And what are you who live within the world
except a picture of the Son of God in broken pieces,
each concealed within a separate and uncertain bit of
clay?* (text, pp. 554f)

In summary, Level One contrasts the reality of
Heaven with the illusion of the hell that we made. On
this Level the Course makes no compromise between
these two for they cannot both be true. The reality of
one denies the existence of the other, and the Course
teaches that you cannot have a little bit of hell in
Heaven, nor Heaven in hell. This metaphysical position is the foundation for the Course's teaching of forgiveness.

The ego attempts to obscure the difference between Heaven's truth and the world's illusion so as to
fulfill its purpose in keeping the problem of the ego
from God's Answer. The problem to which God created the Holy Spirit as Answer is the belief in the reality of the dream, which is in our mind. By removing
itself from the mind the ego succeeds in obfuscating the
Holy Spirit's Voice. The world, and all its problems
which demand our attention, thus distract us from
where the real problem is: our belief in the world and
the separation that gave rise to it. It is not only the
Kingdom of Heaven that is within, but the ego's kingdom as well. The Course summarizes this aspect of the
ego's plan:

> *A problem cannot be solved if you do not know what it is. . . . This is the situation of the world. The problem of separation, which is really the only problem, has already been solved [by the Holy Spirit]. Yet the solution is not recognized because the problem is not recognized. . . .*
>
> *All this complexity [of the world's problems] is but a desperate attempt not to recognize the problem, and therefore not to let it be resolved* (workbook, p. 139).

Before we can discuss the Holy Spirit's answer of forgiveness, however, we must first look at the workings of the split and separated mind as they are manifest in this world of dreams. The unholy trinity of sin, guilt and fear that we described above as an inherent part of the original ego—the Son of God who fell asleep—is retained within each fragmented part of the Sonship. Thus every seemingly separated Son—the individual false selves (or personalities) with which we identify—carries within itself, consciously or unconsciously, the original belief in sin, guilt and fear.

Chapter 6

LEVEL TWO: THE UNHOLY TRINITY—SIN, GUILT, FEAR

As we go through our lives, confronted with the challenges and upheavals on both developmental and daily levels, it is not very practical or helpful to be told that the world and the body with which we are so identified and in which we are invested are mere illusions, the product of a delusionary thought system. Yet the Course repeatedly tells us how practical it is and states, in fact, that

The body is merely part of your experience in the physical world . . . it is almost impossible to deny its existence in this world. Those who do so are engaging in a particularly unworthy form of denial (text, p. 20).

With this in mind we speak of the second level (Level Two) which is outlined in the chart in the Appendix. On this level the world is seen as a classroom in which we learn lessons, and is not dismissed as a mere illusion that we ignore. Rather we are encouraged to "be in the world yet not of it" (John 15:19). Practically speaking, what does this mean? Referring to the chart we see that Level Two consists of the distinction between the "wrong mind" and the "right mind." Both reflect a way of perceiving the physical world based upon an underlying thought system.

Only two choices are open to us: the wrong mind, which is the domain of the ego; and the right mind, which is the home of the Holy Spirit. The goal of the wrong-minded ego is to perpetuate the original sin-guilt-fear syndrome, thereby ensuring the ego's continuity. On the other hand the goal of the right mind, the dwelling place of the Holy Spirit, is to undo wrong-minded thinking through forgiveness and awaken us to the realization that we have never left our Father's house. The Course reminds us: "You *are* a stranger here [this world]. But you belong to Him Who loves you as He loves Himself" (manual, p. 87).

As a choice must be made between these two alternatives we speak also of a third part of this separated mind, the aspect that chooses. In the chart we have called this the "decision-maker." The reader may recall that in Chapter 3 we discussed the sleeping Son of God, and spoke of two voices that were available to him from which he could choose: the Holy Spirit's Voice for God or the ego's voice for guilt and fear. In this and the following chapter we shall discuss the ego thought system, which will enable us to become aware of its dynamics so that we can make another choice, the choice for God. The Course comments that because of the conflict in our mind we choose against the joy that we truly desire:

> *To fulfill the Will of God perfectly is the only joy and peace that can be fully known, because it is the only function that can be fully experienced. When this is accomplished, then, there is no other experience. Yet the wish for other experience will block its accomplishment, because God's Will cannot be forced upon you, being an experience of total willingness* (text, p. 131).

In our presentation of the thought systems of the ego and the Holy Spirit, and the need to choose between the two, we are essentially presenting the positions of the Light and dark groups as they are experienced within the middle group, who will eventually "choose once again" and return Home. It seems clear, incidentally, that like many spiritual paths *A Course in Miracles* is geared towards the middle group, for it is they who experience the conflict between the two voices. The Light group obviously has no need to awaken from the dream, while the dark group members are enjoying the end product of their experiment, quite content that they can destroy what they have made. Their guilt is more deeply repressed than the middle group's and so is far less accessible to examination and correction. When the middle group withdraws its opposition from the dark group, as we shall see in chapter 8, that group too will be healed.

In the Course, incidentally, Jesus cautions us against thinking of the ego as a thing, separate and independent from our minds:

> *I have spoken of the ego as if it were a separate thing, acting on its own. This was necessary to persuade you that you cannot dismiss it lightly, and must realize how much of your thinking is ego-directed. . . . The ego is nothing more than a part of your belief about yourself. Your other life has continued without interruption, and has been and always will be totally unaffected by your attempts to dissociate it* (text, p. 61).

Therefore, having discussed a paradigm for how the world and the individuals therein came to be, we now explore those same dynamics of the ego as they are expressed in individuals: the unholy trinity of sin, guilt and fear, and its impact on each individual psyche.

Contrary to popular belief children are not born into this world innocent. Each child or entity brings with itself all the ontological self-hatred (guilt) and terror from that original instant of separation for which it has not yet forgiven itself. The very fact that it is born into a body witnesses to the seeming reality of what it believes it has done to God and to Christ. Every physical and psychological experience reinforces the ego-body identification, and thus carries with it the grim and painful memory of the original instant of separation.*

Thus we have the basic foundation for the thought system of all who walk this world "uncertain, lonely, and in constant fear" (text, p. 621): We feel we have attacked our Creator and each other by our "sin" of separation, to which separate bodies are the witness. Guilt is the psychological exprience of this belief in sin and can be defined as the total of all our negative thoughts, feelings and beliefs about ourselves. These would include feelings of inadequacy, inferiority, unworthiness, incompetence, incompleteness, shame, self-hatred, and a belief that our wretched state is far beyond the capacity of anyone, including God, to love us. One of the most devastating characteristics of guilt is that it always demands punishment for our "badness." Thus, along with Chicken Little, we live in the world fearful of the "inevitable" punishment that will befall us: "Yesterday was awful, today is terrible, and tomorrow will be unthinkable." The origin of all fear, therefore, regardless of its seeming cause in the world,

---

* The only exception are the isolated examples of a truly enlightened being, what the East calls an avatar or bodhisattva, and the Course a "Teacher of teachers." These would be the members of the Light Group who have accepted the Atonement for themselves, and choose to come into the world of illusion to teach that there is no world. However, as the Course states, these examples are "so rare" that it is hardly necessary to discuss them here.

is the punishment our ego has told us is our just deserts because of our sinfulness, which our experience of guilt must dictate. Sin, guilt and fear thus constitute the basic foundation of the ego's thought system, upon which it now builds what seems to be a massive defensive system against our true Identity as Christ.

In the previous chapter we discussed the ego's use of time on an ontological level to reinforce its emerging thought system of separation from God's eternity. On the individual level we can observe the same dynamics with the same purpose. As long as we believe in the reality of a continuum of time we remain trapped in the ego's spatial-temporal world. The unholy trinity of sin, guilt and fear is the ego's means to accomplish this. The belief in our inherent sinfulness for what we have done in the past leads, as we have seen, to our experience of guilt. Guilt, in turn, results in our fear of the future punishment we believe we deserve. Thus is the ego's world of time made real, with the past and future locked together in a vise of guilt that prevents our choosing the holy instant in the present that would release us, through forgiveness, from the ego's grasp.

Time then is the framework within which the ego carries out its plan against God to ensure its survival. It proceeds in this way: Having convinced us of the reality of our sinful and guilty self the ego leaves us with the belief that at any moment we may be annihilated by the wrathful God we have attacked. Overwhelmed with terror that our loving Creator may destroy us we can only ask the ego's help to alleviate the pain of our fear. The ego responds with what the Course refers to as the "ego's plan for salvation." This plan has two components: denial and projection.

One of Freud's most important contributions was

his description of the unconscious, and its importance in influencing our conscious thoughts, experience and behavior. Nonetheless, most of us do not sufficiently appreciate the extent to which our conscious lives are directed by thoughts we hold in our unconscious and therefore are not aware of. St. Paul expressed this situation rather poignantly in exclaiming: "For the good that I would I do not: but the evil which I would not, that I do" (Romans 7:19). We in a more psychologically sophisticated age can better understand this dilemma, recognizing the dynamic of denial (used by the Course synonymously with repression). As Freud remarked that the goal of psychoanalysis was to make the unconscious conscious, so too does the Course have as its goal the undoing of the fear that leads to the repression of what the ego has judged to be dangerous.

We have already described the amount of terror that was experienced in the seeming separation from God. No one can walk this world with that amount of fear in their conscious awareness. Therefore, the split mind of the ego pushes the memory of this seeming event into the unconscious, magically hoping like the frightened ostrich that what cannot be seen (or remembered) is no longer there. As the Course states, in the context of the ego's belief that it is at war with God:

> Forget the battle. Accept it as a fact, and then forget it. Do not remember the impossible odds against you. Do not remember the immensity of the "enemy," and do not think about your frailty in comparison. Accept your separation, but do not remember how it came about. Believe that you have won it, but do not retain the slightest memory of Who your great "opponent" really is (manual, p. 43).

We may liken our guilt to an iceberg, whose

greater bulk lies below the surface of the water so that all that is visible is the tip. Analogously, our conscious experience of guilt is but the tip of a far greater experience of immense self-hatred that we are not even aware of, having pushed it into the unconscious. The Course teaches that "Nothing that you have refused to accept can be brought into awareness" (text, p. 42). Thus, the ego completes its first part of the plan to "save" us from our guilt by counseling us to push it out of awareness, pretending that what we have made real is no longer there.

However, the repressed guilt has not really gone anywhere, and remains lurking within our mind, waiting as it were for the moment to strike our consciousness. Thus, the ego has a second tactic in its plan to protect us from the onslaught of our guilt and fear: projection. We have already seen this dynamic at work in the making of the world. In that ontological instant the middle group listened to the voice of the ego, turned its back on the message of the Light group, and sought to deny its own believed culpability in the separation by placing the blame on the dark group. This projection of the thought of separation in opposition to the dark group, to state it once again, led to the emergence of the physical world of separation.

On an individual level we replicate the same dynamic. Unable to tolerate the pain of our own self-hatred (guilt) we follow the ego's counsel not to see it within, but in someone else (projection). Thus we have taken our perceived guilt, first denied it in ourselves and then placed it outside. In this way the ego has convinced us we have successfully escaped our guilt. As the Course states:

The world but demonstates an ancient truth; you will believe that others do to you exactly what you think you did to them. But once deluded into blaming them you will not see the cause of what they do, because you want *the guilt to rest on them. How childish is the petulant device to keep your innocence by pushing guilt outside yourself, but never letting go! It is not easy to perceive the jest when all around you do your eyes behold its heavy consequences, but without their trifling cause* (text, p. 545).

However, what the ego has not told us is that its plan of salvation from guilt is the perfect way of holding on to it. Projection of guilt, as we shall explore in greater depth in the following chapter, always entails attack. We seek to blame another for what we are secretly blaming ourselves for, although this can take different forms. However, on some level we know that our attack is unjustified since its cause, regardless of the external circumstances, rests with our unconscious desire to avoid looking at our own ego self. Thus our attack cannot but make us even guiltier.

And so the circle is complete: We begin with our guilt, which we then deny and project, only to feel guilty over these attacks of projection. This is the guilt-attack cycle which is the ego's major tactical weapon in its war against God. Of such is the ego's plan for salvation, which the Course describes in this way:

The ego always tries to preserve conflict [i.e., guilt]. It is very ingenious in devising ways that seem to diminish conflict, because it does not want you to find conflict so intolerable that you will insist on giving it up. The ego therefore tries to persuade you that it can free you of conflict, lest you give the ego up and free yourself (text, p. 120).

The ego's plan for salvation centers around holding grievances. It maintains that, if someone else spoke or acted differently, if some external circumstance or event were changed, you would be saved. Thus, the source of salvation is constantly perceived as outside yourself. Each grievance you hold is a declaration, and an assertion in which you believe, that says, "If this were different, I would be saved" (workbook, p. 120).

Elsewhere, the Course depicts the more sophisticated form in which the ego acts out its plan. It is reminiscent of our myth, and we quote from part of the Course's description:

A brother separated from yourself, an ancient enemy, a murderer who stalks you in the night and plots your death, yet plans that it be lingering and slow; of this you dream. Yet underneath this dream is yet another, in which you become the murderer, the secret enemy, the scavenger and the destroyer of your brother and the world alike. Here is the cause of suffering, the space between your little dreams and your reality. The little gap you do not even see, the birthplace of illusions and of fear, the time of terror and of ancient hate, the instant of disaster, all are here. Here is the cause of unreality. And it is here that it will be undone.

You are the dreamer of the world of dreams. No other cause it has, nor ever will. Nothing more fearful than an idle dream has terrified God's Son, and made him think that he has lost his innocence, denied his Father, and made war upon himself (text, p. 542).

Projection of guilt takes two basic forms, what the Course refers to as special hate and special love relationships. In the following chapter we shall examine the specific dynamics of special relationships, and see how both result in reinforcing the guilt that is crucial to the ego's existence.

Chapter 7

SPECIAL RELATIONSHIPS: THE PSYCHOLOGY OF THE MIDDLE GROUP

Special Hate Relationships

If we search honestly within ourselves, as the Course repeatedly asks, we cannot help recalling to mind our special hate relationships. These would include not only the people whom we hate and attack, past and present, but also the organizations, institutions, religions, political and economic systems, other nations—their policies and leaders—whom we hold responsible for our personal and collective ills. This hatred or anger takes many forms, ranging from the mild to the extreme:

> The anger may take the form of any reaction ranging from mild irritation to rage. The degree of the emotion you experience does not matter. You will become increasingly aware that a slight twinge of annoyance is nothing but a veil drawn over intense fury (workbook, p. 32).

It is essential to the ego's plan for salvation that there be enemies, onto whom we can project our hatred and then attack. Without them we are forced to confront our hatred of ourselves, which the ego has already convinced us would mean certain annihilation. In order to survive, therefore, the ego tells us we must have an enemy, someone we can blame for the misery and unhappiness that is ultimately our own responsibility. This inevitably gives rise to a perception of a

"We-They" world, peopled with "good guys" and "bad guys," victims and victimizers. Thus we continually identify ourselves with the innocent victims of the world, who suffer unjustifiably at the hands of evil and dark forces beyond their control. All the while our guilt—"evil and dark"—remains hidden in the shrouded vaults of our unconscious, forever protected by our "justified" anger at the world outside.

> *Anger always involves projection of separation, which must ultimately be accepted as one's own responsibility, rather than being blamed on others. Anger cannot occur unless you believe that you have been attacked, that your attack is justified in return, and that you are in no way responsible for it. Given these three wholly irrational premises, the equally irrational conclusion that a brother is worthy of attack rather than of love must follow. What can be expected from insane premises except an insane conclusion? The way to undo an insane conclusion is to consider the sanity of the premises on which it rests. You cannot be attacked, attack has no justification, and you are responsible for what you believe* (text, p. 84).

Throughout the span of recorded time we call history abundant evidence exists to demonstrate how the ego thought system has operated. Perceiving separation and lack, different cultures, societies, tribes and empires, considering themselves deprived, ended up attacking others whom they considered outsiders. All the while these aggressors justified their attacks under the guise of various rationalizations, including economic imperatives, political necessities and "holy wars."

Let us recall to mind once again, since this chapter is on middle group psychology, that from the very moment of separation the middle group, given the ego's plan for salvation, had to perceive the dark group as outside themselves. Therefore it should come as no surprise that these attack thoughts have been ongoing from the separation until the present time. Since that ancient instant all our experiences have been colored with the red drops of blood that have flowed from the Son's original belief that he had slain his Father and Source. The pages of history literally drip with this blood, which is but the symbol of the original attack thought against God. This grim description finds a parallel in this striking passage from the Course that depicts the ego's religion of murder and death:

> To know reality is not to see the ego and its thoughts, its works, its acts, its laws and its beliefs, its dreams, its hopes, its plans for its salvation, and the cost belief in it entails. In suffering, the price for faith in it is so immense that crucifixion of the Son of God is offered daily at its darkened shrine and blood must flow before the altar where its sickly followers prepare to die (workbook, p. 457).

We are presently experiencing an age where, because of our advanced technology, communication is practically instantaneous. It is very instructive, as we watch the news on television or read about it in the daily papers, to see the all-inclusive nature of this middle group psychology that pervades the population, nations and leaders, of the entire planet. Projection makes perception: Our perception of world affairs can be boiled down to this equation:

> The individual middle group psychology we retain within our mind, plus the ideological and national middle group psychology we were taught, equals our

91

world view which is a projection of the false self concept we have made.

Because of our identification with the ego's plan for salvation all of us are seeking to find those scapegoats we can safely attack with impunity, hiding behind the "face of innocence" that allows us to identify with the "good" against the "bad." We do this with individuals, but also with various groups: family, religious, community and national. Moreover, all groups but play out on a collective scale these ego dynamics of the individual:

> *And so this face [of innocence] is often wet with tears at the injustices the world accords to those who would be generous and good. This aspect never makes the first attack. But every day a hundred little things make small assaults upon its innocence, provoking it to irritation, and at last to open insult and abuse . . . is it not a well-known fact the world deals harshly with defenseless innocence?* (text, p. 610)

Because of the false self concept we have constructed and our need for self-interest as protection, shared interests become obliterated. The outcome of this scenario engenders tremendous fear throughout the seemingly fragmented parts of the Sonship for we unconsciously believe—"Guilt demands punishment"—that others will attack us as we have attacked them. Thus we are kept glued to the hypnotism of our misperceptions. "My country (religion, tribe, empire, etc.) right or wrong" has been the clarion call of every group since the inception of the separation, holding high the banner of self-interest that flaunts the triumph over God and the unity of the Sonship. Such attack on others is then rationalized by our need to defend ourselves against counter-attack, and the ego cycle of attack-defense has begun:

The world provides no safety. It is rooted in attack . . . (and) gives rise but to defensiveness. For threat brings anger, anger makes attack seem reasonable, honestly provoked, and righteous in the name of self-defense. . . . Attack, defense; defense, attack, become the circles of the hours and the days that bind the mind in heavy bands of steel with iron overlaid, returning but to start again. There seems to be no break nor ending in the ever-tightening grip of the imprisonment upon the mind (workbook, p. 277).

There is a passage in *A Course in Miracles* whose implications, if taken seriously, are literally mind-boggling. If honestly considered their meaning would eventually lead to freedom and salvation. The text states:

To learn this course requires willingness to question every value that you hold. Not one can be kept hidden and obscure but will jeopardize your learning. No belief is neutral. Every one has the power to dictate each decision you make. For a decision is a conclusion based on everything that you believe (text, p. 464).

Discussing the illusory nature of our problems, the workbook makes the same point:

Perhaps you will not succeed in letting all your preconceived notions go, but that is not necessary. All that is necessary is to entertain some doubt about the reality of your version of what your problems are (workbook, p. 140).

This is the "little willingness" that is referred to elsewhere in the Course as the only thing asked of us by the Holy Spirit.

As an exercise in honesty, therefore, we can carefully begin to search our minds with the willingness to question every value that we hold. At first glance this might appear as a facile exercise. However, as we begin to do it we will inevitably realize the enormous resistance we have to question our sacrosanct assumptions—values that we have assumed as our self identity and ego personality. There are many different approaches to pursuing this exercise. The following are two examples: From when we awaken in the morning to when we go to sleep at night we can make a decision to monitor all thoughts, words and deeds with the goal of viewing the investments we have in certain values. An alternate exercise is to list on paper all the values that we hold in the following categories: personal and professional relationships, religious and spiritual beliefs, and political, economic and social values. After listing all our conscious values we can then proceed to question why we indeed uphold these values. As the Course teaches, we should always ask this one question of everything in the world: "What is it for? What is its purpose? What is the meaning of what I behold?"

Let us suppose that because of our belief system and conditioned mind one of our political values is the elimination of an ideological system in all its forms, East or West. It would be instructive to investigate why we as a nation intensely dislike other ideological, political or economic systems different from our own. Why, as a nation and as individual citizens, do we have such an investment in ridding the world of any ideology that we deem as unworthy, evil and to be feared? When did God appoint us as His supreme commanders, generals and first lieutenants to enforce laws and values that *He never established*? This is a supreme example of middle group mentality, so all-pervasive that almost no one has escaped from it.

In any of its forms nationalism is clearly based on the We-They psychology of the middle group, and thus it is easy to understand the inevitablity of its almost universal adoption throughout history. Just as on an individual level the special hate relationship sustains the ego system that spawned it, so too does its nationalistic expression fulfill the same purpose on a larger scale. The ego's survival is ensured, even at the "expense" of the destruction of the external world.

"What is it for? And what is the outcome of such a nationalistic position in our individual lives?" First and foremost it provides a wonderful scapegoat onto whom we project our guilt, and by opposing any "ism" as an "evil" we make the error of separation real in our minds. This of course is exactly what the ego wants. Furthermore, opposing the "opposers"— as for example opposing war through peace activities with an attitude of hatred and separation—also makes the error of separation real and thus can be an entrapment as well. One should never underestimate the subtlety of the ego.

When it comes to religious values we find the exact same dynamic in observing the judgments made on the atheist, non-believer or heretic, from subtle theological pronouncements to outright condemnation. Regardless of the form of these judgments the outcome remains the same: the exclusion of some of God's children from His Kingdom. Here is middle group psychology in its most blatant form, posing as a message of concern, love and salvation by self-appointed ministers of God against all those who do not believe *their* truth and the "Word of God." This division, disunity, hatred and attack but reflect the original middle group mentality that made the sin of separation real and split the Sonship into "good" and "bad," "light" and "dark," "holy" and "unholy," and "saved" and "damned." Once again, members of the middle group have presumed for themselves the position of God's chosen spokespersons and defenders of the faith. In contrast the Light group would have us look beyond the errors of both dark *and* middle group members, as we see in the following message:

> *Dream softly of your sinless brother, who unites with you in holy innocence. And from this dream the Lord of Heaven will Himself awaken His beloved Son. Dream of your brother's kindnesses instead of dwelling in your dreams on his mistakes. Select his thoughtfulness to dream about instead of counting up the hurts he gave. Forgive him his illusions, and give thanks to him for all the helpfulness he gave. And do not brush aside his many gifts because he is not perfect in your dreams. He represents his Father, Whom you see as offering both life and death to you* (text, p. 543).

Special Love Relationships

The same exercise we discussed above under special hate—subjecting all our values to the criterion of "What is it for?"—is also relevant to those relationships the Course calls special love. In a world of diverse multiplicity we are apt to exclude these special love relationships from the scrutiny asked of us. Yet it is these relationships that are the most effective weapons in the ego's arsenal, justifying the Course teaching that they are the home of guilt and but a thin veil drawn over the face of special hate. Special love relationships—from the least to the most intimate—are attempts to keep our guilt and self-hatred out of awareness and thus avoid the seering pain such awareness would bring. The starting point here is a belief in scarcity, i.e., that there is a profound unwholeness or lack that we feel in ourselves. This is an essential aspect of our experience of guilt. The Course explains the scarcity principle in the specific context of the separation:

> While lack does not exist in the creation of God, it is very apparent in what you have made. It is, in fact, the essential difference between them. Lack implies that you would be better off in a state somehow different from the one you are in. Until the "separation," which is the meaning of the "fall," nothing was lacking. There were no needs at all. Needs arise only when you deprive yourself. You act according to the particular order of needs you establish. This, in turn, depends on your perception of what you are. . . . [The] sense of separation would never have arisen if you had not distorted your perception of truth, and had thus perceived yourself as lacking (text, p. 11).

Obviously we do not wish to walk around consciously feeling that there is something inherently wrong or incomplete about ourselves. Furthermore, we have made a strong individuality or self concept that shields us from this awareness. It is this self concept of sin and guilt, whose unconscious center is the belief in lack, that is the most sacred citadel in the ego's kingdom. This false self we have made uses and manipulates relationships to fulfill its own perceived neurotic needs, not realizing that using and manipulating others constitutes an attack on them, thereby reinforcing the guilt we have cleverly sequestered to the unconscious realm.

Briefly, special love relationships are those in which we allow ourselves to become dependent on other people as a way of substituting for our dependence on God. Rather than turning to Him, or the Holy Spirit, for the solution to our perceived problem of lack, guilt and self-hatred, we seek to surround ourselves with special love relationships that will "protect" us from confronting this guilt. The Course comments:

> No one who comes here but must still have hope, some lingering illusion, or some dream that there is something outside of himself that will bring happiness and peace to him. If everything is in him this cannot be so. And therefore by his coming, he denies the truth about himself, and seeks for something more than everything, as if a part of it were separated off and found where all the rest of it is not. This is the purpose he bestows upon the body; that it seek for what he lacks, and give him what would make himself complete. And thus he wanders aimlessly about, in search of something that he cannot find, believing that he is what he is not (text, p. 573).

However, these relationships never truly undo our guilt; rather the special love relationship makes guilt real in our mind by making real the need to develop dependent relationships that will defend ourselves from the pain of our guilt. We use others as a cover so that we no longer consciously experience guilt's painful presence.

Our "love" for another is thus contaminated by our need to have others provide us with a more acceptable self concept that is the opposite of the unacceptable ugly image we cannot bear to look at. That is why the Course states that love without ambivalence is impossible in this world. Our attractions to other people are colored by this unconscious dependency need to have people like and approve of us—as children, parents, lovers, spouses, pupils, therapists, friends, coworkers, etc. Our love for others therefore is not for who they are—the Christ—but for what they can do for us in terms of fulfilling our ego needs, in whatever form symbolizes the fulfillment of my unconscious demand to shield me from my guilt. This love is thus conditional upon people's capacity to be this special love cover for our guilt.

Special love quickly changes to its underlying hate, however, when our needs are no longer met. As pyschology teaches: Dependency breeds contempt. In other words, I love you as long as you fulfill my expectations and meet my need; but as soon as this need is not met—i.e., either you change, or my perceived needs change—my guilt begins to surface in my conscious mind. Following the ego's plan for salvation my experienced fear and anxiety now lead me to blame you for my discomfort. You have thus become the cause of my unhappiness, shifting from the role of savior to that of enemy. Special love has become the special hate it always was and I am now justified in casting you out as "love partner" and seeking another: "Another can be found" (workbook, p. 319). Everyone on this planet has experienced this dilemma for none of us escapes the most fundamental of all special love or dependency relationships, that of a child to its parents, real or surrogate.

To summarize the dynamics of the special love relationship let us use the following image. Imagine a closet in which is contained the terrifying guilt we cannot bring ourselves to look at. Our conscious mind is in the room outside the closet and wants no part of this psychological darkness. The closet door serves to contain and keep hidden the feared sin and guilt. It is thus imperative that this door remain securely shut, lest our guilt escape into awareness forcing us to deal with its pain and anguish. The closet therefore represents the unconscious wherein our "secret sins and hidden hates" (text, p. 621) are kept. The special love relationship is the door that "protects" us from having to look within the closet of our mind and view the sin and guilt the ego tells us will destroy us.

In conclusion, our special relationships are really mini-wars in which we believe we are fighting against the enemy outside to protect ourselves from the enemy within. In all of them we "but relive the single instant when the time of terror took the place of love" (text, p. 513). Thus each and every special relationship becomes a grim reminder of that instant of separation when we believed in our insanity we had killed God and Christ, and set ourselves upon the throne of creation. The absolute madness of such a belief system is colorfully characterized in the following passage:

> Do you not realize a war against yourself would be a war on God? Is victory conceivable? And if it were, is this a victory that you would want? The death of God, if it were possible, would be your death. Is this a victory? The ego always marches to defeat, because it thinks that triumph over you is possible. And God thinks otherwise. This is no war; only the mad belief the Will of God can be attacked and overthrown. You may identify with this belief, but never will it be more than madness. And fear will reign in madness, and will seem to have replaced love there (text, p. 452).

All our special relationships are thus examples of the middle group mentality which is predicated on the perception of "good guys" (special love—we and our allies in the middle group) and "bad guys" (special hate—dark group). We ally ourselves with those who support our need to project onto an enemy that is perceived to be outside of us. Our special love partners thus enable us to feel good about ourselves, denying our underlying feelings of self-hatred, while our special hate partners provide us with the justification for seeing our hatred outside. This dilemma appears hopelessly insoluble, for our unconscious guilt continually spurs us to form this "endless, unrewarding chain of special relationships" (text, p. 295). These only reinforce the underlying guilt, leading to a seemingly unending vicious cycle which appears to have no way out.

Continually impelled by the ego's savage insanity to protect ourselves *from* ourselves we wage war against the world, sometimes overtly (special hate), sometimes under the guise of love (special love). Behind every attack stands the savage Father we invented, against whose vengeance, we believe in our madness, our special relationships provide defense. Yet behind this invented savagery of God stands yet one final Figure: our loving Creator who has never ceased His Call to awaken us from our insane dream. It is His Love that is screened out by the ego's love, but which calmly waits upon our choice for the forgiveness that will return us to Sanity.

Chapter 8
ACCEPTING THE ATONEMENT

The Course says that the ego's thought system is foolproof but that it is not Godproof. Without God's help, the ego's massive defense against Him—sin, guilt, fear, and special relationships—would indeed be insurmountable. However, God did not leave us without Himself, and His extension into the dream is called the Holy Spirit.

The Holy Spirit is God's loving Presence in our separated and sleeping mind, reflecting the ongoing message of the Light group that there is another way of perceiving what seem to be the overwhelming problems of the world. Choosing to forgive—this "other way of perceiving"—is the means the Holy Spirit uses to awaken us from our dream of judgment and pain. Forgiveness too is a dream, but it is what the Course refers to as the "happy dream" that gently bridges the gap between the ego's nightmares and the awakening to reality. As the Course states:

> So fearful is the dream, so seeming real, he [God's Son] could not waken to reality without the sweat of terror and a scream of mortal fear, unless a gentler dream preceded his awaking, and allowed his calmer mind to welcome, not to fear, the Voice That calls with love to waken him. God willed he waken gently and with joy, and gave him means to waken without fear (text, p. 542).

> The goal the Holy Spirit's teaching sets is just this end of dreams. For sights and sounds must be translated from the witnesses of fear to those of love. . . .

From knowledge, where He has been placed by God, the Holy Spirit calls to you, to let forgiveness rest upon your dreams, and be restored to sanity and peace of mind. Without forgiveness will your dreams remain to terrify you. And the memory of all your Father's Love will not return to signify the end of dreams has come (workbook, p. 427).

Referring to the chart in the Appendix, we note that the right mind, being the dwelling place of the Holy Spirit, is the correction for the nightmare dreams of the wrong-minded ego. Since God placed the Holy Spirit in our mind to help undo our illusions and correct our misperceptions, He is the Comforter, Guide, Teacher, and the Answer to all the seeming problems the ego has invented. As the Voice of the Light group the Holy Spirit is the principle of the Atonement, which is God's correction for our belief that the separation from Him was real. Through the Holy Spirit within our mind the Atonement waits our acceptance, brought about by forgiveness:

The full awareness of the Atonement, then, is the recognition that the separation never occurred (text, p. 90).

The acceptance of the Atonement by everyone is only a matter of time. This may appear to contradict free will because of the inevitability of the final decision, but this is not so. You can temporize and you are capable of enormous procrastination, but you cannot depart entirely from your Creator, Who set the limits on your ability to miscreate (text, p. 18).

The Holy Spirit is this "limit," for His presence in our mind ensures that we can, as the Course states elsewhere, never be totally insane. God's loving presence ensures that at some point everyone will hear His

Call and awaken unto Him. The outcome, as the Course reassures us, "is as certain as God" (text, p. 52).

The mechanism of forgiveness is the miracle, which is defined as the correction for our faulty way of thinking and perceiving; shifting from judgment, condemnation and grievances to forgiveness and joining. The Course explains:

> The miracle does nothing. All it does is to undo. And thus it cancels out the interference to what has been done. It does not add, but merely takes away. And what it takes away is long since gone, but being kept in memory appears to have immediate effects. This world was over long ago. The thoughts that made it are no longer in the mind that thought of them and loved them for a little while (text, p. 547).

Thus the miracle is a shift in perception from the wrong mind of the ego to the correction that is the right mind of the Holy Spirit, a shift that undoes the barriers that keep us separate from each other and ultimately from our Creator and Source. Practically synonymous with the word *miracle*, in the right-minded box of the chart, are *forgiveness*, *Atonement*, *healing*, *salvation* and *true perception*. All these terms are virtually interchangeable with each other.

Remember that the key idea in the ego's thought system, both in its inception as well as in our individual experiences, is that someone else is responsible for the miserable state I am in: everyone and anyone except me. The Course comments:

> The "reasoning" by which the world is made, on which it rests, by which it is maintained, is simply this: "You are the cause of what I do. Your presence justifies my wrath, and you exist and think apart

from me. While you attack I must be innocent. And what I suffer from is your attack" (text, p. 540).

It is this idea of projecting responsibility for our own thoughts, decisions and actions that forgiveness specifically addresses. The Course's understanding of forgiveness is totally different from how the world has thought of it and, one might add, different from two thousand years of Christian teaching and practice. We forgive each other for what has *not* been done to us, not pardoning or overlooking what we believe others have done to us, or to those people or groups with whom we identify. What does this mean?

Forgiveness is fundamentally based on an inner shift in how we see ourselves. If our basic self image is of a vulnerable, guilt-ridden self, an innocent victim caught in a world perceived as threatening and hostile, then we must inevitably also believe that others have done this to us and that they can never be forgiven for these sins committed against us. The Course states:

> *No one can waken from a dream the world is dreaming for him. He becomes a part of someone else's dream. He cannot choose to waken from a dream he did not make. Helpless he stands, a victim to a dream conceived and cherished by a separate mind* (text, p. 541).

However, if we remember our Identity as Christ—hearing the Voice of the Holy Spirit, the Call of the Light Group—then we recognize our inherent invulnerability as sinless children of God. This thus enables us to perceive the situation differently. Rather than making real the projections of our own self-hatred now perceived outside us, the basic mistake of the middle group, we can now recognize the essential illusion of our attempt to make the separation real for ourselves through attacking others:

Illusions about yourself and the world are one. That is why all forgiveness is a gift to yourself. Your goal is to find out who you are, having denied your Identity by attacking creation and its Creator. Now you are learning how to remember the truth. For this attack must be replaced by forgiveness, so that thoughts of life may replace thoughts of death (workbook, p. 103).

The ego sees all situations as consisting of two categories: those who are attacked and those who attack; i.e., victims and victimizers. The Holy Spirit likewise sees two categories, though His are totally without attack and blame. Every situation in the world, in His loving perception, is either an expression of God's Love or else a call for it. Therefore those who seem to be attacking are merely expressing their own self concept of guilt and fear, which they are defending against by following the ego's plan for salvation by attacking someone else. Thus they are calling out for the Love of God that in their ancient memory they believe they denied and are not worthy of:

If only attack produces fear, and if you see attack as the call for help that it is, the unreality of fear must dawn on you. For fear is a call for love, in unconscious recognition of what has been denied (text, p. 202).

The process works this way: We have already noted that the ego always projects its guilt in the form of hatred and attack. Thus the first step in forgiveness is for us to recognize that, as the workbook teaches, we are never upset for the reason we think and that our anger is never justified. We must also recognize that we cannot do this alone. The Course emphasizes that the

Holy Spirit needs only our little willingness to question the validity of our judgments. With His help we withdraw our projection from outside of us back to within us, remembering that *we* are the dreamer of this dream of victimization. Thus we can choose to have a happy dream of forgiveness in which our "enemy" and ourselves are joined in an often unconscious desire to awaken from this dream of hell, rather than be kept different and separated by our ego's projections of guilt and attack.

Once we have withdrawn our projection and accepted full resonsibility as decision-maker for our feelings of separation and hurt, the next step in the process of forgiveness is to ask the Holy Spirit's help to shift our perception of ourselves. Thus we ask not only to forgive the situation but also ourselves. We read in the Course:

> Against the hatred that the Son of God may cherish toward himself, is God believed to be without the power to save what He created from the pain of hell. But in the love he shows himself is God made free to let His Will be done. In each of you, you see the picture of your own belief in what the Will of God must be for you. In your forgiveness will you understand His Love for you; through your attack believe He hates you, thinking Heaven must be hell. Look once again upon your brother, not without the understanding that he is the way to Heaven or to hell, as you perceive him. But forget not this; the role you give to him is given you, and you will walk the way you pointed out to him because it is your judgment on yourself (text, p. 492).

In other words, no mistake that we or others have

made justifies our anger or guilt which, in the ego system, must lead to punishment. As the Course repeatedly teaches, the ego demands that sins be punished while the Holy Spirit only sees mistakes that need correction.

As an example let us take an intimate relationship where we experience ourselves as being wronged and therefore hurt because of what we have judged to be unfair treatment. As students of the Course we recognize that this is another situation in the classroom of our lives to practice forgiveness. Knowing we have an internal Teacher within our minds we make a decision to ask His help. That entails a recognition that our ego feelings of anger, hurt and condemnation are not in our best interests, since "Holding grievances is an attack on God's plan for salvation" (workbook, p. 122).

This process of evaluation requires only a little willingness on our part to question our interpretation of the situation. As the Course asks: "Do you prefer that you be right or happy?" (text, p. 573). Our wrong mind would always want to be "right," but at the expense of our happiness. The ego's "rightness" is always some form of attack and hatred which can only lead to reinforced guilt and pain. The right mind heeds the Course's caution to "Beware of the temptation to perceive yourself unfairly treated" (text, p. 523), and thus chooses the happiness of setting aside judgments of "right" and "wrong" and "victim" and "victimizer." The inevitable result is the joy of remembering the unity of all people, with no exception.

Forgiveness also entails accepting the painful fact that unconsciously we have wanted to be unfairly treated, for this then justifies our self concept of the innocent victim. Without victimizers this concept obviously can not be maintained. Therefore as the Course explains we continually send out messengers of fear to bring back the desired messages that witness to the "reality" of a hostile, uncaring world. Against this world we need constant vigilance and protection which often entails justified feelings of vindictiveness. Thus whether or not we are "responsible" for the actions of others in any given situation we *are* responsible for wanting the unfair treatment, and therefore we are responsible for our reactions of innocence and anger. As the Course states in a very powerful passage:

> *The secret of salvation is but this: That you are doing this unto yourself. No matter what the form of the attack, this still is true. Whoever takes the role of enemy and of attacker, still is this the truth. Whatever seems to be the cause of any pain and suffering you feel, this is still true. For you could not react at all to figures in a dream you knew that you were dreaming. Let them be as hateful and as vicious as they may, they could have no effect on you unless you failed to recognize it is your dream* (text, p. 545).

Our ego has peopled the world with special relationships, as we have already noted. These are the ones we need to forgive, both those we have hated and those we believe we have loved. Turned over to the Holy Spirit these same relationships that have been the home of guilt and have imprisoned us still further in the ego world become transformed by the Holy Spirit into holy relationships; that is, relationships whose purpose has been shifted from guilt to forgiveness, from unholiness to holiness:

> *The holy relationship . . . is the old, unholy [special] relationship, transformed and seen anew. The*

holy relationship is a phenomenal teaching accomplishment. In all its aspects, as it begins, develops and becomes accomplished, it represents the reversal of the unholy relationship (text, p. 337).

The holy relationship reflects a *process* of forgiveness, in which people's usual experience is to alternate between specialness and holiness in their relating; one moment holding grievances, the next letting them go, only to pick them up again later. The Course employs the term "holy instant" to denote the interval of time when we choose the miracle of forgiveness instead of attack and grievances, a holy relationship to take the place of specialness:

The holy relationship is the expression of the holy instant in living in this world. Like everything about salvation, the holy instant is a practical device, witnessed to by its results. The holy instant never fails. The experience of it is always felt. Yet without expression it is not remembered. The holy relationship is a constant reminder of the experience in which the relationship became what it is (text, p. 337).

All that is asked of you is to make room for truth. You are not asked to make or do what lies beyond your understanding. All you are asked to do is let it in; only to stop your interference with what will happen of itself; . . . The holy instant is not an instant of creation, but of recognition. For recognition comes of vision and suspended judgment. . . . Undoing is not your task, but it is up to you to welcome it or not (text, p. 419).

Yet again, this is an instant we must continually choose until it becomes as habitual as breathing, and the holy instants increase so that our entire day becomes one single holy instant of forgiveness. This is the attitude and vision that constitutes the Course's goal of the real world.

However, the ego does not take such shifts lying down. Having previously allied ourselves with the ego's plan for salvation, our shift in allegiance to the Holy Spirit is seen by the ego as an act of betrayal and a declaration of war. Here is where, as the Course explains, the ego can turn from suspiciousness to viciousness (text, p. 164). Later the text comments on the experienced discomfort we feel as we change the goal in our relationships from guilt to forgiveness:

> In the transition there is a period of confusion, in which a sense of actual disorientation may occur (text, p. 322).

> At once His goal replaces yours. This is accomplished very rapidly, but it makes the relationship seem disturbed, disjunctive and even quite distressing (text, p. 337).

In a discussion of the six stages in the development of trust, the manual includes four that entail some amount of discomfort. These include periods of undoing, sorting out, relinquishment and unsettling (manual, pp. 8-10). In all of these we experience the fear we have been taught by the ego to associate with listening to the Holy Spirit and returning to God. As we choose to listen to His Voice of love and forgiveness the ego seeks to remind us of the punishment that will be forthcoming because of our sin against God.

> The ego is, therefore, particularly likely to attack you when you react lovingly, because it has evaluated you as unloving and you are going against its judgment. The ego will attack your motives as soon as they become clearly out of accord with its perception of you. . . . The ego will make every effort to recover

111

and mobilize its energies against your release (text, pp. 164,166).

It requires patience and practice to learn, over time, to recondition our minds to associate peace with God and pain with the ego.

An integral part of the Holy Spirit's curriculum for us—the plan of the Atonement—is the development of gratitude for the learning opportunities found in our special relationships. Were it not for these relationships, onto which we have projected our unconscious guilt, we would never have the chance to look at what the ego has kept hidden and, with the Holy Spirit, learn to forgive it. Our attitude therefore should be one of gratitude, not because people have attacked us but because their seeming attack has brought forth what would otherwise have remained forever hidden. Such gratitude on the part of the middle group would have enabled them to look within and forgive their own mistake, rather than believe it rested outside them.

This practice of the holy instant, shifting from the specialness goal of guilt to the holiness goal of forgiveness, is called by the Course our "special function," given us by the Holy Spirit:

> *Such is the Holy Spirit's kind perception of specialness; His use of what you made, to heal instead of harm. To each He gives a special function in salvation he alone can fill; a part for only him. Nor is the plan complete until he finds his special function, and fulfills the part assigned to him, to make himself complete within a world where incompletion rules. . . . Forgiveness is the only function meaningful in time. It is the means the Holy Spirit uses to translate specialness from sin into salvation. . . .*

112

Salvation is no more than a reminder this world is
not your home. . . . And this is seen and understood
as each one takes his part in its undoing, as he did in
making it. He has the means for either, as he always
did. The specialness he chose to hurt himself did God
appoint to be the means for his salvaiton, from the
very instant that the choice was made. His special sin
was made his special grace. His special hate became
his special love [here used in the positive sense] (text,
p. 493).

Fulfillment of one's special function of forgiveness
leads to what the Course calls the vision of Christ or
true perception, in which

The grace of God rests gently on forgiving eyes,
and everything they look on speaks of Him to the be-
holder. He can see no evil; nothing in the world to
fear, and no one who is different from himself. And as
he loves them, so he looks upon himself with love and
gentleness. He would no more condemn himself for
his mistakes than damn another. He is not an arbiter
of vengeance, nor a punisher of sin. The kindness of
his sight rests on himself with all the tenderness it
offers others. For he would only heal and only bless.
And being in accord with what God wills, he has the
power to heal and bless all those he looks on with the
grace of God upon his sight (text, p. 492).

The learning of forgiveness as practiced in our
special relationships occurs in the classroom of our individual lives. Thus *A Course in Miracles* is stated in cur-
ricular terms. Its goal, like that of any teacher, is to
have its students eventually generalize its lessons. We
are encouraged by the Course to practice our forgiveness lessons with all our individual learning partners so
as to learn one day the curriculum goal that there is

nothing to be forgiven—in others or ourselves: The separation from God never truly happened except in dreams which had no effect on Reality. Thus the purpose of *A Course in Miracles* is to have us integrate its teaching so that every single moment of our lives—from birth to death, morning to evening—is perceived as "another situation where God's gift [the vision of Christ] can once again be recognized as ours" (text, p. 621). This gift is offered us whenever we are tempted to accuse another of sin. The Course reminds us:

Your brother's sinlessness is given you in shining light, to look on with the Holy Spirit's vision and to rejoice in along with Him. . . . Be willing, then, to see your brother sinless, that Christ may rise before your vision and give you joy (text, p. 412).

Relating what we have discussed in this chapter to the myth, we read the following from the Course:

Truth is restored to you through your desire, as it was lost to you through your desire for something else. Open the holy place that you closed off by valuing the "something else," and what was never lost will quietly return. It has been saved for you (text, p. 412).

In the myth we read that the Light group continually attempted to remind the middle group of the difference between truth and illusion, and that to oppose illusion was to make it real in their minds. The "something else" that the middle and dark groups had chosen was simply not there in Reality. Its presence warranted nothing more than a smile at the silly, mad idea that presumed to make a substitute for God and Heaven. This reflects the Course teaching about not making the error real, which opposition must always do. The lesson for us is clear: Whenever we feel tempted to oppose anyone or anything we are once again falling into the ego's trap of making illusions real and therefore Reality false. The Course asks us to join our "gentle laughter" with the Holy Spirit as we look together on what seems to cause us and others pain:

> *Perhaps you come in tears. But hear Him say, "My brother, holy Son of God, behold your idle dream, in which this could occur." And you will leave the holy instant with your laughter and your brother's joined with His* (text, p. 545).

The temptations in our world to make the error (the separation) real are legion, ranging from concern over nuclear war, sadness and rage at the Holocaust, or our reactions to the almost daily news accounts of rapes, murders, and thefts. We are tempted in our personal lives as well, by dozens and dozens of problematic situations—major and minor—that arise daily. Perceiving victims and victimizers in situations that seem to cry out for intervention of some kind would appear to be the normal human response. But how normal is it to render the Sonship broken into fragments, each one at war with the next, and believe that our loving Creator is helplessly standing by, powerless to stop the injustices of the world He supposedly created?

It is easy to empathize with the middle group members pleading with the Light group to do something to stop or prevent the atrocities of the ego's world. However, we repeat the Course's counsel: "Trust not your good intentions. They are not enough" (text, p. 355). The history of the world's futility to find an end to injustice is the witness to the impossibility of combatting illusions with illusion, opposition with opposition, attack with counterattack. The Course teaches, in words that could very well have come from the Light group:

How does one overcome illusions? Surely not by force or anger, nor by opposing them in any way. Merely by letting reason tell you that they contradict reality. They go against what must be true. The opposition comes from them, and not reality. Reality opposes nothing. What merely is needs no defense, and offers none. Only illusions need defense because of weakness. And how can it be difficult to walk the way of truth when only weakness interferes? You are the strong one in this seeming conflict. And you need no defense (text, p. 445).

Truth does not fight against illusions, nor do illusions fight against the truth. Illusions battle only with themselves. Being fragmented, they fragment. But truth is indivisible, and far beyond their little reach. You will remember what you know when you have learned you cannot be in conflict. One illusion about yourself can battle with another, yet the war of two illusions is a state where nothing happens. There is no victor and there is no victory. And truth stands radiant, apart from conflict, untouched and quiet in the peace of God (text, pp. 453f).

It is thus only by rising "above the battleground" of illusions, looking back on the insane dream below, that we can truly become instruments of peace. Peace does not come through opposing but only by "denying the denial of truth"; in other words, not reinforcing the ego's denial of God by making attack and pain real. The Course therefore deals with our attitudes and perceptions—*how* we see the world—and not with our behavior. Since the Course so clearly teaches that the world is illusory—"There is no world! This is the central thought the course attempts to teach" (workbook,

p. 237)—it would make no sense for it to make pronouncements about interventions in a world that does not exist.

On the other hand we have already spoken of the Course's emphasis on its practicality, and so it is not necessarily true that we do not *do* anything in the face of what appears to be attack or injustice. The Course does offer guidelines for living in this ego world, but these deal with uncluttering our mind from the ego's "raucous shrieking" that prevents us from hearing the Holy Spirit's Voice, who *does* guide us. Thus the Course does not advocate standing by while one person's call for love is expressed through the form of attack. However, it does advocate not judging the "attacker." Rather we are asked to look beyond the form of the "attack" to its cause, the underlying guilt and call for love shared by all the separated Sonship. Guilt and fear—the ego's interference—can only be undone by forgiveness and love. Our angry thoughts of opposition do not solve the problem for they but reinforce the belief in separation that *is* the problem. It is our attitude of judgment that needs correction and not someone else's behavior:

> The Holy Spirit does not teach you to judge others, because He does not want you to teach error and learn it yourself. He would hardly be consistent if He allowed you to strengthen what you must learn to avoid. In the mind of the thinker, then, He is judgmental, but only in order to unify the mind so it can perceive without judgment. This enables the mind to teach without judgment, and therefore to learn to be without judgment. The undoing is necessary only in your mind, so that you will not project, instead of extend (text, p. 101).

Withdrawing our opposition from those we have judged as evil—e.g., members of the dark group—we in effect deny the reality of their sin, not to mention our own. Without the strength of the shared illusion of having made the error real, the thought of sin and guilt in ourselves and others disappears back "into the nothingness from which it came" (manual, p. 32). That is the power of forgiveness, and of such is the Kingdom of Heaven on earth.

Remembering the myth where the middle group turned its back on the Voice of the Light group, we see that it was the judgment placed on the dark group that prevented the return to Sanity. Judging another as evil or sinful is tantamount to judging ourselves, as we have already discussed. At that instant of judgment a veil falls before our eyes and we are blinded to truth, a wall of static arises and we are deaf to the Voice of forgiveness. Thus we are urged to give up judgment for this is "the obvious prerequisite for hearing God's Voice . . . a fairly slow process" (manual, p. 25). Moreover,

> When you react at all to errors, you are not listening to the Holy Spirit. He has merely disregarded them, and if you attend to them you are not hearing Him (text, p. 155).

Despite our consistent judgments and attacks upon ourselves and others, we are told that the Holy Spirit "still calls you to return, and He will be heard when you place no other gods before Him" (text, p. 173). These "other gods" are anything and everything in the ego system, and are judgments so strongly held in our mind that the Course cautions that "only very few can hear God's Voice at all" (manual, p. 30).

In summary, then, when we find ourselves in situations that scream of injustice—personal or collective—and we seek to take action in the world, the Course would ask us first to go within and ask for help to remove the blocks of judgment that would prevent our hearing the Voice that would guide us. The Course urges us, finally: ". . . seek not to change the world, but choose to change your mind about the world" (text, p. 415).

Thus it is that in each and every moment of our lives we are given the opportunity of healing our mind, not only in this instant of individual consciousness but in that timeless instant of terror in which we are still choosing to forget who we are. They are the same instant, for all

> Trials are but lessons that you failed to learn presented once again, so where you made a faulty choice before you now can make a better one, and thus escape all pain that what you chose before has brought you. In every difficulty, all distress, and each perplexity Christ calls to you and gently says, "My brother, choose again." He would not leave one source of pain unhealed, nor any image left to veil the truth. He would not leave you comfortless, alone in dreams of hell, but would release your mind from everything that hides His face from you. His holiness is yours because He is the only Power that is real in you. His strength is yours because He is the Self That God created as His only Son (text, p. 620).

Turning away from our judgment of the sin of others who would oppose God, we listen finally to the Voice of Truth and Love that has never ceased to call to us from the instant we chose to deafen our ears. Letting go our thoughts of opposition we find they are

119

replaced for us by the awareness of unity that was always there, waiting for our remembrance. Our perception now is healed and peace has come to us at last. We have attained the real world, our final step in the Atonement.

Chapter 9

AWAKENING FROM THE DREAM: THE RETURN HOME

The Course states that "Knowledge is not the motivation for learning this course. Peace is" (text, p. 128). In other words the Course's goal is not the state of Heaven, where only knowledge abides. Rather its goal is to have us live in this world, our minds transformed into a state of pure forgiveness which translates into an experience of total peace. This transformation is the attainment of what the Course refers to as the real world.

Practicing this Course therefore does not lead to avoiding or departing this physical world, and the Course offers these consoling words to those who have this concern:

> Fear not that you will be abruptly lifted up and hurled into reality. Time is kind, and if you use it on behalf of reality, it will keep gentle pace with you in your transition (text, p. 322).

Instead the Course urges us to live in this physical world, but to do so with a completely transformed perspective of reality. This is the vision of Christ that contains only holy thoughts of the oneness of God's Son.

> When you have looked on what seemed terrifying, and seen it change to sights of loveliness and peace; when you have looked on scenes of violence and death, and watched them change to quiet views of gardens under open skies, with clear, life-giving water running happily beside them in dancing brooks that never

waste away; who need persuade you to accept the gift of vision? And after vision, who is there who could refuse what must come after? Think but an instant just on this; you can behold the holiness God gave His Son. And never need you think that there is something else for you to see (text, p. 414).

The real world is actually accepting the Holy Spirit's happy dreams instead of the nightmares of the ego:

Accept the dream He gave instead of yours. . . . Rest in the Holy Spirit, and allow His gentle dreams to take the place of those you dreamed in terror and in fear of death. He brings forgiving dreams, in which the choice is not who is the murderer and who shall be the victim. In the dreams He brings there is no murder and there is no death. The dream of guilt is fading from your sight, although your eyes are closed. A smile has come to lighten up your sleeping face. The sleep is peaceful now, for these are happy dreams (text, pp. 542f).

The real world too is illusory, for it corrects what never happened. Yet it is the one illusion that leads beyond them all. The real world is a symbol for the opposite of what we have made and represents our acceptance of the Holy Spirit's perception, the awareness of the Light group. It is the sign that total forgiveness has come for the ego has been relinquished, no longer serving any purpose:

How lovely is the world whose purpose is forgiveness of God's Son! How free from fear, how filled with blessing and with happiness! And what a joyous thing it is to dwell a little while in such a happy place! Nor can it be forgot, in such a world, it is a little while till timelessness comes quietly to take the place of time (text, p. 573).

Therefore living in the real world would be the equivalent of joining the Light group, nevermore to become entrapped in the middle or dark group's illusory world of opposition. All lingering thoughts of hatred toward oneself or anyone else vanish, and love for all living things becomes our only awareness. This shift entails a total letting go of all judgments of others and oneself, which is the prerequisite for peace:

> *You have no idea of the tremendous release and deep peace that comes from meeting yourself and your brothers totally without judgment* (text, p. 42).

The state of the real world is what the Course refers to as the "reflection of holiness."

> *In this world you can become a spotless mirror, in which the holiness of your Creator shines forth from you to all around you. You can reflect Heaven here. Yet no reflections of the images of other gods must dim the mirror that would hold God's reflection in it* (text, p. 271).

The "other gods," as we have seen, are the ego's idols we have made to substitute for God—our values, cherished self-concepts and "sacred cows"—and that we have held as a veil between ourselves and the Holy Spirit.

We have come as far as learning goes and through our forgiveness have completed our part in the Atonement. What lies beyond this step individually is also beyond all learning:

> *Yet even forgiveness is not the end. Forgiveness does make lovely, but it does not create. It is the source of healing, but it is the messenger of love and not its Source. Here you are led, that God Himself can take*

the final step unhindered, for here does nothing inter-
fere with love, letting it be itself. A step beyond this
holy place, a step still further inward but the one you
cannot take, transports you to something completely
different. Here is the Source of light; nothing per-
ceived, forgiven nor transformed. But merely known.
This course will lead to knowledge, but knowledge
itself is still beyond the scope of our curriculum. Nor
is there any need for us to try to speak of what must
forever lie beyond words. We need remember only that
whoever attains the real world, beyond which learning
cannot go, will go beyond it, but in a different way.
Where learning ends there God begins, for learning
ends before Him Who is complete where He begins
and where there is no end (text, p. 369).

When every last member of the middle and dark
groups attains the real world and joins the Light
group, hearing no other Voice but the Holy Spirit, the
fragmented Sonship is reunited in what the Course de-
fines as the Second Coming, a definition differing from
the traditional expectation of the return of Jesus.

The First Coming of Christ is merely another
name for the creation, for Christ is the Son of God.
The Second Coming of Christ means nothing more
than the end of the ego's rule and the healing of the
mind (text, p. 58).
The Second Coming is merely the return of sense . .
the awareness of reality (text, pp. 158f).
It is a part of the condition that restores the never lost,
and re-establishes what is forever and forever true. It
is the invitation to God's Word to take illusion's
place; the willingness to let forgiveness rest upon all
things without exception and without reserve. . . .
Forgiveness lights the Second Coming's way, because

it shines on everything as one. And thus is oneness recognized at last. . . . The Second Coming is the time in which all minds are given to the hands of Christ, to be returned to spirit in the name of true creation and the Will of God (workbook, p. 439).

The Second Coming therefore is the correction for the Sonship's mistaken thinking, the awakening from the dream of separation. It restores to awareness the innocence that had been given by God in creation, the innocence whose unity *seemed* to be forever lost. Now is the fragmented mind healed and the Holy Spirit's purpose complete:

The Second Coming ends the lessons that the Holy Spirit teaches, making way for the Last Judgment, in which learning ends in one last summary that will extend beyond itself, and reaches up to God (workbook, p. 439).

The Last Judgment, not to be confused with the traditional Christian understanding of God's punishing the bad and rewarding the good, is the Course's term for the penultimate step in the journey. It is the final judgment the Sonship makes between truth and illusion. The Course states:

The Last Judgment is generally thought of as a procedure undertaken by God. Actually it will be undertaken by my brothers with my [Jesus] help. It is a final healing rather than a meting out of punishment. . . . The Last Judgment might be called a process of right evaluation. It simply means that everyone will finally come to understand what is worthy and what is not (text, p. 30).

The Second Coming ushers in the Last Judgment and allows the Sonship finally to hear the Voice that called to it from the beginning:

Christ's Second Coming gives the Son of God this gift: To hear the Voice for God proclaim that what is false is false, and what is true has never changed. And this the judgment is in which perception ends. At first you see a world that has accepted this as true, projected from a now corrected mind. And with this holy sight, perception gives a silent blessing and then disappears, its goal accomplished and its mission done (workbook, p. 445).

At the Last Judgment the now reunited Sonship takes one final look at what it had made and recognizes that

Nothing the Son of God believes can be destroyed. But what is truth to him must be brought to the last comparison that he will ever make; the last evaluation that will be possible, the final judgment upon this world. It is the judgment of the truth upon illusion, of knowledge on perception: "It has no meaning, and does not exist." (text, pp. 508f).

The Final Judgment on the world contains no condemnation, for it sees the world as totally forgiven, without sin and wholly purposeless. Without a cause, and now without a function in Christ's sight, it merely slips away to nothingness. There it was born, and there it ends as well. And all the figures in the dream in which the world began go with it. Bodies now are useless and will therefore fade away, because the Son of God is limitless (workbook, p. 445).

It is this acceptance of Reality, *as it is*, that undoes the original error. With this recognition the Son awakens from the dream with these holy words upon his lips:

"I am God's Son, complete and healed and whole, shining in the reflection of His Love. In me is His

126

*creation sanctified and guaranteed eternal life. In me
is love perfected, fear impossible, and joy established
without opposite. I am the holy home of God Himself. I am the Heaven where His Love resides. I am
His holy Sinlessness Itself, for in my purity abides
His Own"* (workbook, p. 469).

In response the Son hears his Father say the
words he never thought he would hear again:

*"You are still My holy Son, forever innocent, forever
loving and forever loved, as limitless as your Creator,
and completely changeless and forever pure. Therefore
awaken and return to Me. I am Your Father and you
are My Son."* (workbook, p. 445).

One final "step" remains, although as the Course
states it is not a step at all. It is the gift of God by which
the

*memory of Him awakens in the mind that asks the
means of Him whereby its sleep is done. . . . This
the gift by which God leans to us and lifts us up,
taking salvation's final step Himself. All steps but
this we learn, instructed by His Voice. But finally He
comes Himself, and takes us in His Arms and sweeps
away the cobwebs of our sleep. . . . It restores all
memories the sleeping mind forgot; all certainty of
what Love's meaning is* (workbook, 313).

In a moving passage Jesus ecstatically calls to us
to make the choice that would return us Home:

*O my brothers, if you only knew the peace that will
envelop you and hold you safe and pure and lovely in
the Mind of God, you could but rush to meet Him
where His altar is. Hallowed your name and His,
for they are joined here in this holy place. Here He
leans down to lift you up to Him, out of illusions into
holiness; out of the world and to eternity; out of all*

127

fear and given back to love (manual, p. 82).

In the final pages of the Course we read this prayer of gratitude for our return to what was never truly left:

> *Let us wait here in silence, and kneel down an instant in our gratitude to Him Who called to us and helped us hear His Call. And then let us arise and go in faith along the way to Him. Now we are sure we do not walk alone. For God is here, and with Him all our brothers. Now we know that we will never lose the way again. The song begins again which had been stopped only an instant, though it seems to be unsung forever. What is here begun will grow in life and strength and hope, until the world is still an instant and forgets all that the dream of sin had made of it* (manual, p. 87).

EPILOGUE

The Course teaches that the Holy Spirit was the principle of the Atonement, but that it nonetheless had to be set into motion (manual, p. 85; text, p. 16). In other words the principle that the separation was only a bad dream had to be lived out for the world. It had to be demonstrated that the world of pain and death was nothing more than the product of the Son's misthought that he had attacked and even destroyed his Father. Even more to the point, the Son's belief that God could never forgive his sin, let alone love him, had to be disproved by a perfect demonstration of this love in the face of attack.

It was Jesus who set this Plan into motion and, as he states in the Course, became its head (text, p. 6; manual, p. 85). He was the living manifestation of Heaven's Love, even in the face of what appeared to be its destruction. In this sense Jesus was the symbol of God, for his life of perfect love appeared to be the victim of the world's attack; his seeming death replicating the original separation of the Son's attack on his Father's perfect Love. The entire script of separation, including the making of the world, directly followed upon the belief of both the middle and dark groups that the impossible had indeed occurred, with very real effects. The middle group's guilt over its "sin" of turning against the Love of Heaven held this belief in place. This guilt in turn was held in place by the ego's fear of God's retaliatory vengeance that made Love impossible. All was lost for the Son now believed he had destroyed Love forever.

"Into this hopeless and closed learning situation, which teaches nothing but despair and death" (manual, pp. 1f), Jesus came to teach we were mistaken—not sinful, simply mistaken in what we believed. In his own person and through his life he re-enacted for the sleeping Sonship the dream of its betrayal of God's Love. The great cosmic drama that occurred in that one mad instant was here brought into the world of time and space and played out in bold strokes, to be relived by all who believed in the reality of dreams.

Buried in the consciousness of the middle group was the terrifying memory of its sin and God's disfavor, and it was this memory that was stirred by the events in Palestine two thousand years ago. However, now there was a difference. Because the presence of God had come into the world, in the person of Jesus, a different memory was resurrected in our awareness. This memory, also deeply buried, was of the Light group's gentle insistence that the Son's judgment was wrong: There was indeed another way of looking at the mistaken thought of separation.

Thus the crucifixion of Jesus not only brought to the Son's awareness the thoughts of sin, guilt and fear, but also the thought of Atonement. Here at last was incontrovertible proof that God was not angry at the "sin" of the world. In the face of the symbolized murder of God's Love on Calvary was a response of total non-opposition. Confronted by the viciousness of the egos of the world Jesus simply stood back and loved: the perfect manifestation of the Light group's original message:

Do not oppose. . . . Love, our true state, can
never oppose. Love simply is, and there can be no
opposite. What appears as opposite is unreal, and
therefore insane. Do not believe in what does not exist.

Not seeing attack but only the call for love that is born of fear, Jesus could only love and call us to remember who we were, as in these words from the Course:

Child of God, you were created to create the good,
the beautiful and the holy. Do not forget this. The
Love of God, for a little while, must still be expressed
through one body to another, because vision is still so
dim (text, p. 12).

Jesus' body was such a vehicle for us all. In a passage written at Christmas he said:

The Prince of Peace was born to re-establish the condition of love
by teaching that communication remains unbroken even if the body
is destroyed. . . . The lesson I was born to teach, and still would
teach to all my brothers, is that sacrifice is nowhere and love is
everywhere (text, pp. 305f).

Elsewhere, he exhorts us to

Teach not that I died in vain. Teach rather that I did
not die by demonstrating that I live in you (text, p.
193).

Therefore when in each and every circumstance we feel tempted to "perceive ourselves unfairly treated" by the world; when we feel justified in not only being angry, but on a deeper level justified in believing that we deserve unfair treatment because of our unfair treatment of God and Christ, Jesus asks us to remember his teaching lesson and his love. We are not asked to replicate the form of Jesus' lesson of non-opposition, but we *are* asked to model ourselves after its meaning and demonstrate that he lives in us through our forgiveness: loving all people as he loved all people.

Jesus' love for us is the love of God for what He created. Our acceptance of that love awakens us from our dream of betrayal and returns to God the Son that never truly left his Father's House. That love need not be specifically identified with Jesus for us to awaken from the dream, but his example of forgiveness needs to be lived by us if the nightmare is to end. The message of the Light group not to make the error real was repeated from the Cross and echos once again in *A Course in Miracles*. The hope of peace in the world lies in our acceptance of this message, with no reservation and no exception.

Jesus has brought to our weary eyes a "vision of a different world, so new and clean and fresh" (text, p. 621) that to look at the dream-world we have made through this vision cannot but bring tears of joy that we were wrong and God was right. How gladly now we pay the "price" of sacrificing our world for His; a world of murder, terror and hatred exchanged for the real world of joy, love and peace! How grateful we have become that the nightmare was a dream, and that we were never left alone but have been gently awakened by the Voice of Love! And how our hearts soar in joyful thanksgiving that we can return at last with all of Christ as one! Together as one Son our voices unite in one Voice, joined in a grateful chorus of love, from love to Love:

> Let us go out and meet the newborn world, know-
> ing that Christ has been reborn in it, and that the
> holiness of this rebirth will last forever. We had lost
> our way but He has found it for us. Let us go and bid
> Him welcome Who returns to us to celebrate salvation
> and the end of all we thought we made. The morning

star of this new day looks on a different world where
God is welcomed and His Son with Him. We who
complete Him offer thanks to Him, as He gives
thanks to us. The Son is still, and in the quiet God
has given him enters his home and is at peace at last
(manual, pp. 87f).

APPENDIX: CHART

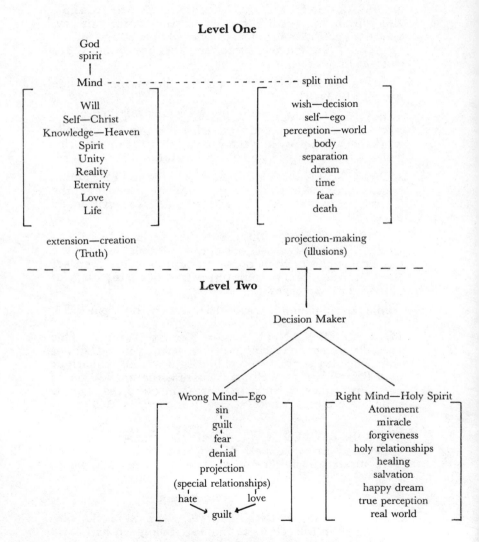

Level One

God
spirit
|
Mind - split mind

Will	wish—decision
Self—Christ	self—ego
Knowledge—Heaven	perception—world
Spirit	body
Unity	separation
Reality	dream
Eternity	time
Love	fear
Life	death

extension—creation   projection-making
(Truth)   (illusions)

Level Two

Decision Maker

Wrong Mind—Ego   Right Mind—Holy Spirit

sin	Atonement
guilt	miracle
fear	forgiveness
denial	holy relationships
projection	healing
(special relationships)	salvation
hate love	happy dream
guilt	true perception
	real world

135

Related Material on **A Course in Miracles**
by Kenneth Wapnick
Available fro| © Foundation for "A Course in Miracles" |Miracles"
P.O. B| RD #2, Box 71, Roscoe, NY 12776 |7

GLOSSARY-INDEX FOR "A COURSE IN MIRACLES,"
2nd edition, enlarged: Summary of the Course's theory;
126 terms defined and indexed; index of over 800 scriptural
references; line-gauge included to assist use of index. 312
pages. $16.

Print-out of added material to first edition; includes line
gauge. $1.50.

THE FIFTY MIRACLE PRINCIPLES OF "A COURSE IN
MIRACLES": Combined and edited transcript of two
workshops of line by line analysis of the fifty miracle principles, supplemented by additional material. 153 pages. $8.

A TALK GIVEN ON "A COURSE IN MIRACLES": Edited
transcript of a workshop summarizing the principles of the
Course; includes story of how the Course was written. 55
pages. $4.

CHRISTIAN PSYCHOLOGY IN "A COURSE IN MIRA-
CLES": The first two sections of this pamphlet present the
basic principles of the Course; the final section discusses
these in the context of some of the traditional teachings of
Christianity. 36 pages. $3.

Audio tape of pamphlet recorded by Kenneth Wapnick. $5.

FORGIVENESS AND JESUS, by Kenneth Wapnick: This
book discusses the teachings of Christianity in the light of
the principles of the Course, highlighting the similarities
and differences, as well as discussing the application of
these principles to important areas in our lives such as
injustice, anger, sickness, sexuality and money. 340 pages.
$16.

THE OBSTACLES TO PEACE: Edited transcript of tape
cassette album by Kenneth Wapnick; line by line analysis of
"The Obstacles to Peace" and related passages. 200 pages.
$12.

Video Cassette Album

SEEK NOT TO CHANGE THE COURSE: Reflections on
"A Course in Miracles": 135 minute talk given by Gloria
and Kenneth Wapnick, including questions and answers,
on some of the more common misunderstandings about
the Course. VHS $30.

Audio Cassette Albums

Recorded Seminars

THE SIMPLICITY OF SALVATION: Intensive overview of the Course. 8 tapes. $65.

HOLY IS HEALING: Psychotherapeutic applications of the Course. 8 tapes. $65.

ATONEMENT WITHOUT SACRIFICE: Christianity, the Bible and the Course. 2 tapes. $15.

THE END OF INJUSTICE: Overview of the Course. 6 tapes. $45.

THE EGO AND FORGIVENESS: Introductory overview of the Course. 2 tapes. $15. (Album consists of first two tapes of "The End of Injustice.")

THE GIFTS OF GOD: The inspired poetry of Helen Schucman, scribe of the Course; album includes personal reminiscences of Helen. 3 tapes. $24.

Line by line analysis of key sections in the Course

THE FIFTY MIRACLE PRINCIPLES: 3 tapes. $24.

THE WORLD ACCORDING TO "A COURSE IN MIRACLES": 3 tapes. $24.

THE OBSTACLES TO PEACE: 6 tapes. $48.

SPECIAL RELATIONSHIPS — PART I: 8 tapes. $65.

SPECIAL RELATIONSHIPS — PART II: 6 tapes. $48.

TIME ACCORDING TO "A COURSE IN MIRACLES": 6 tapes. $48.

JESUS AND "A COURSE IN MIRACLES": 5 tapes. $40.

CAUSE AND EFFECT: 8 tapes. $65.

PSYCHOTHERAPY: PURPOSE, PROCESS AND PRACTICE: 7 tapes. $56.

All prices include shipping, New York State residents please add local sales tax. Order from:

Fo   "

© Foundation for "A Course in Miracles"
RD #2, Box 71, Roscoe, NY 12776

A Course in Miracles may be ordered from:
Foundation for Inner Peace
P.O. Box 635
Tiburon, CA 94920

Hardcover: $40   Softcover: $25

Gloria and Kenneth Wapnick are co-founders, and Vice-President and President of the Foundation for "A Course in Miracles." The Foundation was begun in 1983 to further understanding of the Course through publications, tapes, workshops held nationally and internationally, and a Teaching and Healing Center.